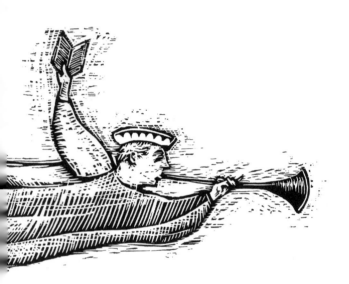

Alma 1–29: *a brief theological introduction*

This publication was made possible by generous support from the Laura F. Willes Center for Book of Mormon Studies, part of the Neal A. Maxwell Institute for Religious Scholarship at Brigham Young University.

Published by the Neal A. Maxwell Institute for Religious Scholarship, Brigham Young University, Provo, Utah. The copyright for the 2013 text of The Book of Mormon is held by The Church of Jesus Christ of Latter-day Saints, Salt Lake City, Utah; that text is quoted throughout and used by permission.

Printed in the United States of America

ISBN: 978-0-8425-0024-1

LIBRARY OF CONGRESS CONTROL NUMBER: 2020902755

Alma 1–29

a brief theological introduction

BRIGHAM YOUNG UNIVERSITY

NEAL A. MAXWELL INSTITUTE

PROVO, UTAH

Kylie Nielson Turley

The Book of Mormon: brief theological introductions series seeks Christ in scripture by combining intellectual rigor and the disciple's yearning for holiness. It answers Elder Neal A. Maxwell's call to explore the book's "divine architecture": "There is so much more in the Book of Mormon than we have yet discovered. The book's divine architecture and rich furnishings will increasingly unfold to our view, further qualifying it as *'a marvelous work and a wonder.'* (Isaiah 29:14) . . . All the rooms in this mansion need to be explored, whether by valued traditional scholars or by those at the cutting edge. Each plays a role, and one LDS scholar cannot say to the other, *'I have no need of thee.'"* [1] (1 Corinthians 12:21)

For some time, faithful scholars have explored the book's textual history, reception, historicity, literary quality, and more. This series focuses particularly on theology—the scholarly practice of exploring a scriptural text's implications and its lens on God's work in the world. Series volumes invite Latter-day Saints to discover additional dimensions of this treasured text but leave to prophets and apostles their unique role of declaring its definitive official doctrines. In this case, theology, as opposed to authoritative doctrine, relates to the original sense of the term as, literally, reasoned "God talk." The word also designates a well-developed academic field, but it is the more general sense of the term that most often applies here. By engaging each scriptural book's theology on its own terms, this series explores the spiritual and intellectual force of the ideas appearing in the Latter-day Saints' "keystone" scripture.

Series authors and editors possess specialized professional training that informs their work but, significantly, each takes Christ as theology's proper end because he is the proper end of all scripture and all reflection on it. We, too, "talk of Christ, we rejoice in Christ, we preach of Christ...that our children may know to what source they may look for a remission of their sins" (2 Nephi 25:26). Moreover, while experts in the modern disciplines of philosophy, theology, literature, and history, series authors and editors also work explicitly within the context of personal and institutional commitments both to Christian discipleship and to The Church of Jesus Christ of Latter-day Saints. These volumes are not official Church publications but can be best understood in light of these deep commitments. And because we acknowledge that scripture demands far more than intellectual experimentation, we call readers' attention to the processes of conversion and sanctification at play on virtually every scriptural page.

Individual series authors offer unique approaches but, taken together, they model a joint invitation to readers to engage scripture in their own way. No single approach to theology or scriptural interpretation commands pre-eminence in these volumes. No volume pretends to be the final word on theological reflection for its part of the Book of Mormon. Varied perspectives and methodologies are evident throughout. This is intentional. In addition, though we recognize love for the Book of Mormon is a "given" for most Latter–day Saint readers, we also share the conviction that, like the gospel of Jesus Christ itself, the Book of Mormon is inexhaustible.[2] These volumes invite readers to slow down and read scripture more thoughtfully and transformatively. Elder Maxwell cautioned against reading the Book of Mormon as "hurried tourists" who scarcely venture beyond "the entry hall."[3] To that end, we dedicate this series to his apostolic conviction that there is always more to learn from the Book of Mormon and much to be gained from our faithful search for Christ in its pages.

—The Editors

Contents

Introduction

This book's invitation is quite simple: read a few Book of Mormon stories that you have probably read before and see them in a new light. As you think about what those stories mean, you will be thinking about God. That, at its most basic, is theology, which means that many of us do theology every day. But theology is not enough. Scripture invites us not only to *think* about God but also to believe and to be changed. We are supposed to *live* differently because of what we believe. In the Book of Mormon, theology is hiding in the stories.

Readers who engage with the Book of Mormon's stories will find themselves changed. This is important to understand. Stories are powerful. A story throws open the door and invites us to come in. It welcomes us to make ourselves at home—and most of us do. We read ourselves into the story, identifying with a character and acting alongside him or her, even when that story is sad, lonely, or upsetting. After vicariously experiencing someone else's story, we are different. People who read stories are transformed in a deeper way and for a longer time than people who read lists of commandments.[1]

The problem with stories is that if we read them without thinking, they may impact us without our knowledge. Careful readers choose to understand how narratives are acting on them, how the stories might alter them. They set aside knee-jerk emotional responses or rash, reactive thinking. Instead of thinking without feeling or feeling without thinking, a careful reader's heart and mind will work together. The resulting interpretations of stories may change a reader's emotions, thoughts, and behaviors, but the reader will be aware of why and how that is occurring.

The Book of Mormon should change readers because this scripture is narrative from the moment Nephi introduces himself until the moment Moroni bids us farewell. Our scripture is an epic tragedy, and many of the stories in Alma 1–29 are about loss. By chapter 29, every person in Nephite society has cause to mourn: lands are lost, peace is lost, faith is lost, conscience is lost, lives are lost, loved ones are lost.

These are only a few of the theological topics in Alma 1–29. Limitations in space, time, and my own perspective make complete coverage in this theological introduction impossible. I did not even try. My study of Alma ☞ began years before this particular project did, and my interpretations are admittedly my own.[2] I have chosen to show respect for scripture by reading slowly, considering words and even punctuation seriously, and contemplating what these elements convey. This approach guided me to compose this book in two sections: the first section explores Alma's experiences on a personal level, analyzing his encounters with the loss and sorrow created by sin. Many assume they know this story, but they may find themselves more shocked by Alma's wickedness, more inspired by his change, and more devastated by the consequences than they expect. The second section explores the Nephite community's experience with the loss and sorrow created by widespread death and destruction, which is also a universal experience but one that is felt

☞ Although other volumes in this series use numerical subscripts to differentiate between people who have the same name, such as Alma₁ or Alma₂, this book only uses subscripts when necessary for clarification. All other references to Alma in this book refer to Alma₂, the son of Alma, who is also called Alma the Younger. Similarly, all references to Mosiah refer to Mosiah₂, the son of King Benjamin.

individually. How scriptural communities and individuals respond to pervasive tragedy and to traumatic harm can model possible approaches to inspired healing for modern readers.

If we engage with scripture, we should prepare ourselves for loss, as well. We may lose a superhuman scripture hero, an idol untouched by doubt or despair and unaffected by circumstances. Depending on your current theologies, you might need to rethink your definition of faith, your assumptions about forgiveness, and your suppositions that Alma's "O that I were an angel" message is an upbeat missionary motivational speech. Readers may lose the comforting assurances that they understand repentance, judge righteously, and know Book of Mormon stories backward and forward. Even then, there is more to lose: Do readers place limits on how "bad" someone can be and still repent? Do they approach mourning casually or another's grief indifferently? Do they believe that God will not require more than a person can handle? If so, these readers may lose their surety. God can request incredible sacrifices, and he does so in these stories. Alma was in pain. We are in pain. Trite, slick solutions are far too flimsy to mend what is broken in our hearts and minds. But the stories in Alma 1–29 are not trite or slick or flimsy. They offer more than theological Band-Aids.

That is good because real people have real problems, and they need real solutions from a real God. The challenge for us as readers is to open our ears and hear, open our eyes and see. Can we read these stories slowly and pause mindfully? Learn of loss and allow ourselves to feel it? And then pause again, feel deeper, ponder longer, and begin to understand? You may find surprising hope in the depths.

PART I

Chapters 1-3

To say that every story needs a beginning, a middle, and an end seems obvious—but Alma might disagree. Alma's life narrative is comprised of multiple small stories and is far from a chronological plot with an introduction, predictable rising action, climax, falling action, and a tidy resolution. Instead, readers are introduced to this man and his life story in a brief, two-verse summary. An angel appears, Alma repents dramatically, and he seemingly moves forward into a life of meaningful service (see Mosiah 27:8, 9). His life concludes with a retelling of his conversion in chiastic poetry in Alma 36 and another, much shorter, retelling in Alma 38. The retold conversion story flips Alma's life story backward and inside out: his life in the Book of Mormon ends with its beginning, begins with its middle, and tells a story (in the middle) that drags through multiple endings, eventually moving beyond the retold beginning that seems like the ending. Alma's story as told in the Book of Mormon is like a circling time warp.

Even more confusing is that the way Alma's story is chronicled allows readers to read smoothly over the time warp. Alma's life is vividly depicted in more than one hundred pages of scripture, more than forty-five chapters, and in 19,777 personal words.[1] Conversion bookends Alma's life and creates closure, that feeling of satisfaction and completeness readers expect to feel when they finish a good book. Biblical authors created closure with the same technique, regularly placing "poetic repetitions at the end of a prose narrative."[2] Because the conversion creates closure around such a lengthy amount of text, readers can be lulled into thinking that they understand Alma. They know his stories and speeches; they read them in the first half of the book of Alma. But the timing in Alma's story is problematic.

The first three chapters of this book mimic the circularity of Alma's conversion story, seeking to understand why this particular story is told multiple times and what impact that retelling might have. Chapter 1 questions our assumptions about Alma's age and the narrative timing of the story. It finds that the narrative timing is symbolic and purposeful in the context of a covenant religion. Chapter 2 returns to Alma's beginnings to explore the beliefs and practices of the unbelievers and to demonstrate that postconversion Alma is clearly and carefully rejecting these beliefs in his public speeches. Chapter 3 considers how Alma's unbelieving past redefines events and relationships throughout Alma 1–29. Without a direct statement clarifying the implications of Alma's preconversion beliefs on his postconversion life, interpretations of Alma can vary, but dates, diction, and descriptions indicate that Alma is a mature and very wicked unbeliever. Readers who see only a rebellious adolescent may misunderstand Alma's speeches and misinterpret his encounters with dissenters.

1

His Course Is One Eternal Round

Many readers know Alma's conversion story, which they would summarize more or less as follows: Alma was a teenage rabble-rouser living a destructive, riotous life with his friends, the wild sons of King Mosiah. But then he encounters an angel, abruptly halts his rebelliousness, grows up, and becomes a responsible citizen and a righteous man like his father, who was the high priest of the church of God. That story is emotionally compelling, fairly predictable, and relatively undemanding. Such stories are typical enough that they garner their own name in the literary world: coming-of-age narrative or *bildungsroman*. This short coming-of-age conversion story is told in Mosiah 27 and then retold in beautifully worded, chiastic poetry in Alma 36. Alma is the hero, the protagonist who takes a quick journey from misguided youth to repentant adult believer, and who then remains unfalteringly righteous for the rest of his very long textual life.

This version of the story may be true. Artists regularly depict Alma as an irresponsible adolescent when the angel appears. Lesson manuals, commentaries, and Church members discuss "Alma the Younger," though the Book of Mormon never uses that name-title, except in the modern study helps, such as chapter headings. Maybe readers are not supposed to know Alma's age when he was converted—yet, date and time references mark the story of $Alma_1$, $Alma_2$, and $Alma_2$'s sons more than any other family in the Book of Mormon. Moreover, some of the timing-related information conveyed is utterly unique to this story. Readers need to account not only for the content that is communicated but also for the fact that someone chose for that content to be communicated in this way in this particular story, and that means questioning assumptions about Alma's age. He may not be as young at the time of his conversion as he has been characterized in Latter-day Saint discourse.

On one hand, a youthful Alma is supported by the substantial series of events that occurs between Alma's conversion and the first year of the reign of the judges. That is the year Alma becomes chief judge, a position he holds for approximately ten years. The question is how much time passes before Alma is chief judge but after he is converted. Mosiah 27–29 describes what occurs, including Alma's and his friends' mission "round about through all the land" (Mosiah 27:32) and Mosiah's translating of the Jaredite plates (Mosiah 28:11). The longer these events take, the greater the likelihood that Alma was young when he was converted. While that idea makes sense in the abstract, the events cannot take up too much time because Mosiah reigns for only thirty-three years. Supposing that the 1–9 year estimate of time[1] between the conversion and the first year of the reign of the judges is somewhat accurate, then a teenaged Alma is only thirty-two to thirty-eight years of age when he disappears a mere nineteen years later (Alma 45:19). A greater length of time between his conversion and the first year of the reign of the judges allows for the possibility that he is older when he exits the story, younger when he converts, or both—but that length of time is bounded by what has to happen in king Mosiah's reign before Alma₁ and his people arrive in Zarahemla. It gets complicated quickly.

The first year of the reign of the judges is the critical year in Alma's life: both Alma₁ and Mosiah₂ die, at ages eighty-two and sixty-three, respectively (Mosiah 29:44–46). In that same year, Alma is appointed chief judge. This means that Alma's father is most likely between seventy-three and eighty-one years old when Alma is converted. This information is surprising, but more surprising is the fact that this is the only time in the entire Book of Mormon that readers learn of age at death. Perhaps this was the only time writers had access to such information. That seems unlikely, but if so, then why was this date recorded so carefully, and why was it included? If there were other times when age of death was available, why is this the only time such information was provided? Either way, the information raises questions about why this family is dated with such specificity. It allows readers to justifiably wonder, How old is the wayward son when his eighty-one-year-old father prays for him? Even if readers assume a long gap between conversion and the first year of the reign of the judges, Alma$_1$ is a seventy-three-year-old father when the angel appears to his son.

Alma could still be young, since elderly men can and do have very young children, but that situation usually leads to an atypical, lengthy gap between the natural deaths of father and son. Readers cannot confirm that hypothesis because Alma's disappearance occurs nineteen years after his father's death. However, Alma's disappearance corresponds with the timing of a natural death and the timing of his sons' deaths: Helaman dies sixteen years after his father disappears (Alma 62:52), and Shiblon dies four years after his brother does (Alma 63:10–11), which seems to be regular generational spacing. Like the age at death, the generational age information is singular. Because the Book of Mormon raises age as an issue and does so in ways that are unique to this family and this story, readers should question Alma's age and contemplate how the story changes if our perception of Alma's age changes (see FIGURE 1 for a possible timeline).

Beyond the scattered dates are a plethora of small but important considerations. Alma is never referred to as being youthful, and he is never called "the younger" in the Book of Mormon. The narrator, presumably Mormon, describes preconversion Alma as a "very wicked and an idolatrous *man*" and a "*man* of many words," suggesting that he was an adult (Mosiah 27:8; my emphasis). While Alma is generally described in the past tense, occasionally he is described with the use of inceptive verbs: Alma "*became* a very wicked and idolatrous man" (Mosiah 27:8; my emphasis), and he "*became* a great hinderment to the prosperity of the church" (Mosiah 27:9; my emphasis). It is a subtle change, but if it is deliberate, then Alma needs enough time to be one way and then become something else. What Alma became is an incredibly persuasive speaker, which again suggests age. Alma has to be old enough not only to master the art of rhetoric but also to amass a following of many people who listened to and were persuaded by his rhetoric (Mosiah 27:8). Lastly, despite notable exceptions such as Mormon (Morm. 2:1–2), capable adults typically had the leadership roles in Nephite society. When Alma becomes the highest ecclesiastical leader and the highest Nephite political-judicial figure, he almost certainly is an adult.

Age is an issue in Alma's story because the text provides unprecedented clues that Alma is a *man*, not an adolescent. These evidences do not indicate Alma's specific age, but they provide enough evidence to suggest that Alma "the younger" was not young at all when he sought to destroy the church of God (Mosiah 27:10). Moreover, the implication of this evidence is that readers not only *can* ask age-related questions but that they *should*. For example, does it make a difference to know

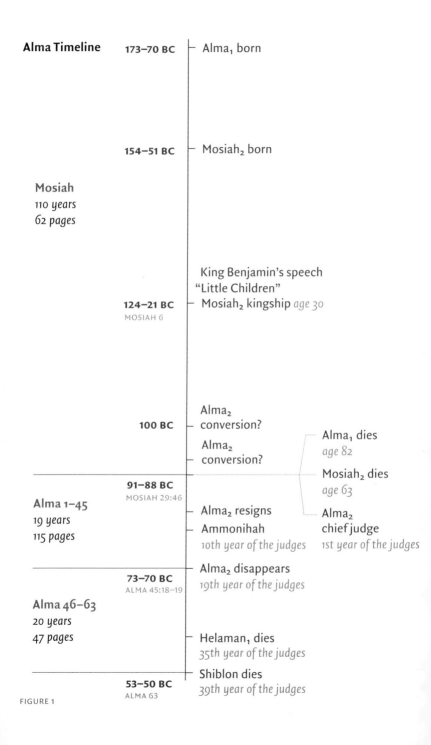

Alma Timeline

173–70 BC ├ Alma₁ born

154–51 BC ├ Mosiah₂ born

Mosiah
110 *years*
62 *pages*

King Benjamin's speech
"Little Children"
124–21 BC ├ Mosiah₂ kingship *age 30*
MOSIAH 6

100 BC ├ Alma₂
conversion?
├ Alma₂
conversion?

┌ Alma₁ dies
age 82

91–88 BC ─── Mosiah₂ dies
MOSIAH 29:46 *age 63*

Alma 1–45
19 *years*
115 *pages*
├ Alma₂ resigns └ Alma₂
├ Ammonihah chief judge
10th year of the judges *1st year of the judges*

73–70 BC ├ Alma₂ disappears
ALMA 45:18–19 *19th year of the judges*

Alma 46–63
20 *years*
47 *pages*
├ Helaman₁ dies
35th year of the judges
├ Shiblon dies
53–50 BC *39th year of the judges*
ALMA 63

FIGURE 1

how old someone is when he or she seriously sins? Does it make a difference how old someone is when he or she repents? Is it easier to trust an adult leader who had some youthful indiscretions (and repented)—or one who spent decades trying to destroy the church as an adult (and repented)? Do readers trust a leader's speeches and advice less if that powerful rhetoric persuaded many to leave the church only a few years previously? Readers may judge, trust, and forgive easier based on age and timing.

When Alma retells his conversion story to his sons, he circles back around to his beginning, creating a story that highlights his age, his repentance, and God's forgiveness. The circling also provides insight into godly time. Chronological time is similar to the beginning-middle-end time of narrative in a linear sense, but chronological time and narrative time differ in progression. Technically, time moves in a steady minute-by-minute progression, whether one is engaged in the most routine of routine tasks or is listening to the once-in-a-lifetime rebuke of an angel. And yet people do not experience time that way, nor do they tell stories chronologically. Psychologists argue that people make "meaning of ...life experiences by punctuating the seamless flow of events and organizing them."[2] In other words, people naturally create stories, breaking up those clock-ticking seconds and replacing them with dramatic rising action, heart-stopping climaxes, and resolutions. Storytellers "lengthen time" with focus and careful description and contract time with descriptive brevity, summary, or even absence. The simple choice of when to start and when to stop the story imposes significance and value on certain events and diminishes others.

Telling stories wrings meaning from the constant flow of time—but the timing in Alma's story does not wring meaning from the world's temporal chronology. Alma's life story in the Book of Mormon does not begin with his birth into linear time but with his rebirth into a new way of life. His story begins when he establishes himself as someone who was "born of God" and embraces a godly life for nineteen years (Mosiah 27:28). His conversion, in Mosiah 27:10–25, is the moment he returns to at the end of his life, the moment Alma thinks will best teach his sons "concerning the things pertaining unto righteousness" (Alma 35:16). In revoicing his conversion moment in Alma 36, he rechooses that critical moment, that choice to listen and repent. Though not discussed in detail, Alma also retells his story in Alma 38:7–8 and Alma 27: 25.

What is the impact of this circular story? Like a perimeter, the conversion story and its poetic retelling form an edge that naturally keeps readers focused on who Alma is inside. Within the boundaries of his conversion narrative, Alma is a chief judge, a high priest of the church of God, and a strong and unflinching confronter of Nehor, Amlici, Korihor, and others. His missionary sermons, as well as his final words to his sons, are filled with brilliant doctrine, powerfully stated. Of course, readers technically know that Alma was wicked before his conversion, but those details are located in the book of Mosiah rather than the book of Alma and are written in a direct characterization style. Alma's preconversion life is downplayed and minimized when the narrator describes Alma abruptly and succinctly as a "man of many words, [who] did speak much flattery to the people …[leading] many of the people to do after the manner of his iniquities" (Mosiah 27:8). The words convey shocking truths, but they summarize rather than dramatize, and the lack of detail shortens narrative time. The way that Alma's story is told prior to his conversion allows these moments to fade to the background.

Then the angel arrives. *How* Alma is portrayed abruptly changes. Suddenly Alma speaks. Unlike the summary of his preconversion self, Alma's conversion story relies on vocalized personal words, sensory details, and action that readers can readily imagine. Instead of being told that Alma speaks powerfully, readers get to judge for themselves: Alma repents aloud and in public, calling his sinful state "the darkest abyss" (Mosiah 27:29) and "an everlasting burning" (Mosiah 27:28) and declaring that he was "wading through much tribulation" and "repenting nigh unto death," before the Lord "[saw] fit to snatch" him from spiritual destruction (Mosiah 27:28). The language is imaginative and imagistic, metaphoric and memorable. Alma's personal words and the description of the angelic manifestation allow readers to create images and engage their minds, and that process intensifies the likelihood of readers remembering these words.

What the words of Alma's story say is meaningful, but *how* the story is told enacts a lesson about God, sin, and repentance—and it does so in comforting ways. Alma teaches in Gideon that God does not have "a shadow of turning ... from that which is right to that which is wrong" and that, therefore, God's "course is one eternal round" (Alma 7:20). In circling around to his beginning, Alma is stepping inside a metaphoric realization of God's time. When Alma retells his story, he is rehearing the angel's rebuke, recommitting himself to repentance, and repeating the moment he cries out for Christ's mercy. He renews his rebirth and reestablishes a choice to live a godly life. Circumscribing a part of his life story with conversion creates a life that ends where it begins and begins where it ends.

Retelling his conversion story may technically return Alma to the middle of his chronological life, but what matters is that it returns Alma to the point when he chooses his new life. The choice to believe is not a singular event. Like a covenant, this moment is relived and rechosen each time it is retold or renewed. Alma's conversion stories circumscribe Alma's godly life, focusing readers on his righteous years and minimizing his past. Who Alma is inside the conversion narratives expands, who he was before his conversion diminishes, and who he can become is left open to possibility.

Alma's angel reappears almost exactly halfway through his godly life, arriving as Alma walks away from his first rejection at Ammonihah. The angel informs Alma that there is "great cause to rejoice." Despite the hardships of the first nine years of the reign of the judges, the angel tells Alma that he "hast been faithful in keeping the commandments of God *from the time which thou receivedst thy first message from [God]*" (Alma 8:15; my emphasis). Although the angel appears when Alma is on his way to his greatest trial and tells him that he should rejoice, and although it is entirely possible that Alma did not begin a life in God until he was much older than he should have been, he can rejoice. It is always the right time to begin living a life in God's time.

2

Numbered Among
the Unbelievers

Mormon does not mince words when he introduces
Alma in Mosiah 27:8. In one short verse, Alma is labeled
as an unbeliever, a speaker of flattery to the people, and
a very wicked and idolatrous man. Most readers readily
acknowledge that Alma was sinful, but understanding
that Alma was an unbeliever is not the same as knowing
what he did or believed to deserve that description. Alma
and others were called unbelievers for distinct reasons,
and moreover, preconversion Alma is also a flatterer,
an idolater, and a very wicked man, labels that parallel
Amalickiah's description. That Alma used these traits to
lead "many of the people to do after the manner of his
iniquities" only exacerbates his sinfulness (Mosiah 27:8).
Is it insensitive or destructive to try to understand preconversion Alma? It can be. However, the same search can
also be wise and even kind. On a practical level, Alma's
teachings and his life story are extensive, and their sheer
length will impact readers who engage. Becoming aware
of who Alma is, what he believes, and how he behaves
helps readers perceive the story's influence. Discerning
Alma's wickedness is also the empathetic basis for discerning the pain behind his interactions, motivations,
and relationships. While the approach could be used to
vilify a beloved scripture figure, understanding Alma's
very wicked beliefs and practices makes him more realistic, his repentance more miraculous, and his redemption more hopeful.

unbeliever

Alma enters the narrative in Mosiah 27. The original chapter, Mosiah XI, is comprised of Mosiah 23–27,[1] thus encompassing what occurs after Alma₁ and his people escape from King Noah, are captured by Lamanites, escape again, and join Zarahemla's melting pot of cultures and people. In Zarahemla, they find multiple groups of people, including the "unbelievers," those "little children" who were too young to comprehend King Benjamin's message (Mosiah 26:1). These children did not enter King Benjamin's covenant. They grew up as a "separate people as to their faith" and remained separate (verse 4). A rough estimate suggests that at the time of Alma's conversion, most are probably between twenty-four and thirty-seven years of age[2] and constitute a larger proportion of Zarahemla's population than do the people of God, due to "dissensions among the brethren" of the church (verse 5).

Alma is described in terms that echo the unbelievers' descriptions, which should not be surprising because Alma is "numbered among the unbelievers" (Mosiah 27:8). When Alma is described as "speak[ing] much flattery," he is doing what other unbelievers do: "deceive many with their flattering words." When Alma leads people "to do after the manner of his iniquities," he is joining other unbelievers who "cause [the people] to commit many sins." His efforts to cause

21

"cause them to commit many sins"
(Mosiah 26:6)

"because of the dissensions among the brethren
they became more numerous" (Mosiah 26:5)

"deceive many with their flattering
words" (Mosiah 26:6)

FIGURE 2 Comparison of Alma and Unbelievers

"much dissension" eventually lead many people out
of the church, similar to the unbelievers whose ranks
swell "because of dissensions among the brethren"—
dissensions provoked by the unbelievers (see FIGURE 2).
Readers may overlook these parallels because the unbelievers and Alma are described in separate chapters in
modern copies of the Book of Mormon. Nevertheless,
Alma is labeled as an unbeliever in the same original
chapter, Mosiah XI, that introduces the unbelievers,
explains their beliefs, and describes their practices. He
is described in similar terms, his practices are parallel,
and the effects of his efforts are the same. It is difficult
to diminish the similarities when they are within the
same story.

The unbelievers define themselves solely in oppo-
sition to the church of God, perhaps because the
entire society except for these children joined King

Beliefs accepted by church, rejected by unbelievers

1	Reject traditions of their Fathers	Mosiah 26:1
2	Reject the coming of Christ	Mosiah 26:2
3	Reject the resurrection of the dead	Mosiah 26:2
4	Reject calling upon the Lord their God	Mosiah 26:4
5	Reject that there should be equality among all men	Mosiah 27:4
6	Reject that priests and teachers should labor with their own hands for their own support	Mosiah 27:5

Practices opposed by church, accepted by unbelievers

7	Practice persecution, especially towards members of the church of God	Mosiah 26:38 27:1–3, 32
8	Practice proselytizing, especially with "flattering words"	Mosiah 26:5–6

FIGURE 3 Unbelievers

Benjamin's covenant (Mosiah 6:2). They reject six beliefs that the church of God accepts, and they agree with two behaviors that members of the church of God are supposed to reject (see FIGURE 3). When the beliefs are listed, readers may question whether Alma could have truly been this misguided, yet Alma's conversion speech directly addresses the beliefs of the unbelievers, seeming purposefully crafted to distance him from his unbelieving past.

In his conversion speech, Alma confesses to the worst of these beliefs and reassures those around him that he has changed. Upon regaining his strength, Alma announces that he has repented of his sins (belief 4). He confesses to his most serious sin and simultaneously announces his new belief: though he previously "rejected [his] Redeemer" (belief 2) and "denied that which had been spoken by [his] fathers" (belief 1), now he knows that the fathers did "foresee that [Christ] will come" (Mosiah 27:30). Interestingly, the dissenters and apostates in the book of Alma connect these beliefs (belief 1 and belief 2). Anti-Christs and unbelievers such as the Amalekites, Korihor, and the Zoramites insist that the Nephite fathers are foolish men who pretend to prophesy, which causes their people to (foolishly) believe in Christ.[3] In his conversion speech, Alma declares that he now knows because of his own visionary experience that the Nephite fathers were right: Christ is real and "will make himself manifest unto all" (Mosiah 27:30).

The specific questions unbelievers have about resurrection are not stated in Mosiah 26 (belief 3). However, Alma speaks about resurrection, explaining in his conversion speech that "at the last day, . . . all men shall stand to be judged," even those "who live without God in the world" (Mosiah 27:31). Ironically, these words answer Ammonihahite attorney Zeezrom's one genuine question. He asks whether "all shall rise from the dead, both the just and the unjust, and [be] brought to stand before God to be judged according to their works" (Alma 12:8). It is obviously impossible that Alma answers Zeezrom's question a decade before it is asked, but the fact that his words are the answer suggests that the conversion narrative addressed a specific issue about the unbelievers' generalized struggles "concerning the resurrection of the dead" (Alma 12:8), a phrase used only by Alma$_1$, unbelievers, and former unbelievers—and Zeezrom.

Alma does not address persecution, flattery, or laboring with his own hands in his conversion speech, although the angel's first words condemn Alma for persecuting the church of God (Mosiah 27:13). Alma's immediate postconversion response to being "greatly persecuted" is mild-mannered "long-suffering" (belief

7) (verses 32–33), his flattering words turn into preaching by imparting and exhorting (verse 33) and by confessing and explaining (verse 35) (belief 8), and he begins "zealously striving" to be an "[instrument] in the hands of God" (verses 35, 36), even if it is unclear whether he is simultaneously laboring with his own hands (belief 6). Nehor arrives in the first year of the reign of the judges sounding like an unbeliever with his claim that "every priest and teacher...ought not to labor with their hands, but that they ought to be supported by the people" (Alma 1:3). Presumably Alma, high priest, is one of the priests who "[return] again diligently unto their labors" after their preaching (belief 6) (Alma 1:26), believing that "the preacher was no better than the hearer...and thus they were all were equal" (belief 5) (Alma 1:26). Alma eventually clarifies conclusively that he has "labored even from the commencement of the reign of the judges until now, with mine own hands" when Korihor accuses him of "glutting on the labors of the people" (belief 6) (Alma 30:31).

Alma rejected his Redeemer, his righteous fathers, repentance, and resurrection. That he and other unbelievers have specific contentions demonstrates that their disagreement with the church of God was theological. Alma was emphatic enough about his beliefs that he chose to "go about secretly," apparently well aware that his efforts to lead people away from the church were "contrary to the commandments of God, or even the king" (Mosiah 27:10). Perhaps he was also looking for the next pleasure party with the sons of Mosiah, but his antagonism was not child's play in terms of belief or outcome. His philosophical disagreement changes this story in critical ways. The conflict in Alma's early story is not a contest between the pious church of God and the hedonistic secular world. It is a clash of theologies, an ideological competition between two groups who are firmly convinced that their respective interpretations of scriptures and their doctrines of deity are correct. The unbelievers reject Christ; they are led by anti-Christs. Members of the church of God embrace Christ; they are led by prophets.

a great hinderment

When Alma enters the story, the clash of theologies is heated and escalating. During the reign of Mosiah, the unbelievers "were not half so numerous as the people of God; but because of the dissensions among the brethren they became more numerous" (Mosiah 26:5). How many people who left the church were lured away with Alma's flattering words? The exact number is unknown, though he "became a great hinderment to the prosperity of the church of God; stealing away the hearts of the people" (Mosiah 27:9). He caused enough dissension that the angel arrives to "convince [him] of the power and authority of God" (Mosiah 27:14) by appearing, shaking the earth, and demanding, "Behold, can ye dispute the power of God?" (verse 15).

This is a critical moment for Alma, a life-changing angelic rebuke that is reported four different times to three different audiences in three different writing genres by two different authors. In Alma 36:11, the angel says to Alma, "If thou wilt be destroyed of thyself, seek no more to destroy the church of God." The most straightforward reading of this sentence is that if Alma wants to be destroyed, then he should seek to destroy the church no more, which obviously does not make sense. Why would Alma quit trying to destroy the church if he wants to be destroyed? The angel should restate either the conditions or the effect: if Alma wants to be destroyed, he should continue destroying God's church; or, alternatively, if he does not want to be destroyed, he should stop destroying God's church.

Scholars have suggested a variety of solutions for this odd statement; they range from assuming scribal error to interpreting this as a Hebraic "uncompleted positive if-[clause] with a negative meaning"[4] to suggesting the addition of "even" or "unless," which would fix the statement by coordinating it more closely with Mosiah 27:16. ☞ Another solution is to fix the punctuation. Because Book of Mormon punctuation was not part of the inspired translation process,[5] this is the simplest justifiable solution:

> "If thou wilt, of thyself be destroyed. Seek no more to destroy the church of God." (Alma 36:9; my punctuation)

> "If thou wilt, be destroyed of thyself. Seek no more to destroy the church of God!" (Alma 36:11; my punctuation)

The angel's words are forthright and firm, and they contrast the magnitude of God's power with the limits of agency. Regardless of Alma's personal desires, he must no longer seek to destroy the church of God. The revised statements align with the angel's first words in Mosiah 27:13: after briefly questioning "why" Alma "persecuteth…the church of God," the angel quotes the Lord as saying, "'This is my church, and I will establish it; and nothing shall overthrow it, save it is the transgression of my people.'"

☞ While these approaches can be solutions, they are each problematic: there is no indication of scribal error in the original or printer's manuscript, the Hebrew phraseology argument requires that readers know Hebrew to understand the face-value meaning of a Book of Mormon sentence in English, and adding in words that make a clause mean its opposite lacks justification: why should one be able to add words that change meaning, and why or when would this rule apply? Notably, Alma's personal writing style uses *if* nearly one hundred times and *even if* just once.

In the Mosiah 27:16 version, the angel commands Alma to "go thy way, and seek to destroy the church no more, that their prayers may be answered, and this even if thou wilt of thyself be cast off." This statement is often read to mean that Alma *should* go his way and quit seeking to destroy the church *or* be cast off. But the angel is not issuing a threat (do this or be destroyed), nor is he stating a conditional (if you do this, then you will be destroyed). There is no *or*, nor is there an *if/then*. The angel's statement should be read as a straightforward imperative without conditions, a reading confirmed when the angel states, "*and this* even if thou wilt of thyself be cast off" (Mosiah 27:16). Alma is told that he must "go his way." The angel mentions no conditions but merely states, "And this"—meaning Alma will go his way— "even if" he chooses to be cast off. Alma understands this phrasing to mean that he will cease destroying the church of God, regardless of personal desire. He understands the angel to say that he has used his last chance. Years later, Alma tells his son, Shiblon, "The Lord in his great mercy sent his angel to declare unto me that I must stop the work of destruction" (Alma 38:7). In this version as in the Mosiah 27 version, there is no *or*, and no conditions; to Shiblon, there is not even an *even if* phrase. Alma understands the angel's words as a simple command or possibly a statement of fact, which parallels the re-punctuated phrasing.

Not only is Alma told straight up to quit destroying the church, but he is aware that God has power to enforce his words. Alma tells Shiblon that the angel demonstrated the power of God in a face-to-face visit, speaking with a voice of thunder that shook the whole earth (Alma 38:7). A quick perusal of the Book of Mormon or a modern news update demonstrates that God regularly allows people to make destructive choices that harm self and others to an ungodly extent. Like he has with so many others, God has allowed Alma astonishing latitude, and Alma used it to persecute church members, lead many people into apostasy, and wreak general havoc on the church of God and its members. But Alma has found God's limit. Whereas Alma's personal salvation may hinge on any number of self-destructive choices, he *must* stop destroying God's church.

very wicked and idolatrous man

At the beginning of his story, Alma is labeled as a "very wicked and an idolatrous man" (Mosiah 27:8). Despite the term's conspicuousness, readers may brush over it, never consciously recognizing that Alma is an idolater. He does not refer specifically to his idol worship, though it seems to have been a problem with others in Zarahemla (see Alma 7:6). Oddly, the Book of Mormon blurs idolatry with *idleness*, explaining that the Nephites "who did not belong to their church did indulge themselves in sorceries, and in idolatry or idleness" (Alma 1:32). Alma 17:15 describes the Lamanites as a "very indolent people, many of whom did worship idols," explaining that idolatrous people want "gold and silver, and precious stones," but they do not want to "labor for them with their own hands" (verse 14). The homophonous connection ties an idol- or idle-worshipping Alma back to the unbelievers and their wish to avoid laboring with their hands (belief 6). In one of the few direct references to idol worship, the Book of Mormon says that the Zoramites' idolatry causes Alma's "heart . . . to sicken" (Alma 31:1). The idol worshipping makes his heart so "exceedingly sorrowful" that he describes the pain as a physical sensation (verse 2).

The grief Alma feels is only exacerbated by watching the Zoramites pray once a week on the Rameumptom, denying Christ (belief 2) (Alma 31:16) and rejecting the "traditions of our brethren" (belief 1) (verse 17). The text says these people are wicked and perverse, like Laban, Sherem, Amlici, Morianton, and others who are *wicked men*. There are only three *very wicked men* in the Book of Mormon: the chief ruler of the Zoramites (Alma 35:8), Amalickiah (Alma 46:9), and preconversion Alma. The leader of the Zoramites is not characterized much further, though Amalickiah and preconversion Alma parallel each other in process, purpose, and outcome. Both use flattery to steal the hearts of righteous people and lead them to do wickedly, and both do this in an effort to destroy the church of God. Both are effective in leading many away to dissension, and both understand that their efforts are tied to the blessings and cursings upon the land according to the Lehite covenant (see FIGURE 4, next page) These generalized labels are sustained by Amalickiah's actions: he provokes civil war among the Nephites in his efforts to be king (Alma 46), and when he is unsuccessful in that endeavor, he murders his way into Lamanite kingship, blames the king's loyal servants, and takes the queen as his wife (Alma 47). Amalickiah recklessly sends the Lamanites to war against the Nephites because he "care[s] not for the blood of his people" (Alma 49:10). In a revealing and repelling moment, he curses God and swears "an oath that he would drink [Moroni's] blood" (Alma 49:27). The particulars behind Amalickiah's general labels create a disturbing image of someone who is indifferent to others' pain, occasionally brutal and vicious, and consistently manipulative. Very wicked is an appropriate descriptor for Amalickiah, but it leaves an unnerving silence. Readers know the horrifying specifics that justify Amalickiah's labels. What specifics justify labeling Alma in parallel terms?

One last parallel deepens the unnerving unknown: Alma 46:10 reports that Amalickiah "led away the hearts of many people to do wickedly; yea, and to seek to destroy

Alma	"a very wicked and idolatrous man" *Mosiah* 27:8	"a man of many words" who "did speak much flattery to the people" *Mosiah* 27:8	"st[tole] away the hearts of the people" as he "led many of the people to do after the manner of his iniquities" *Mosiah* 27:8–9
Amalickiah	"the great wickedness one very wicked man can cause" *Alma* 46:9	"a man of many flattering words" *Alma* 46:10	"led away the hearts of many people to do wickedly" *Alma* 46:10

the church of God, and to destroy the foundation of liberty which God had granted unto them." The wording is awkward enough that Amalickiah might be the performer of all the actions: he might be the one who "led away the hearts" and sought "to destroy" the Nephite religion and liberty. However, parallel structure aligns the infinitive verbs, and that changes the actor from Amalickiah to the people: Amalickiah "led away the hearts of many people to do wickedly," and then, after losing their hearts to Amalickiah's teachings, many people chose "to do wickedly" and chose "to destroy the church of God" and also chose "to destroy the foundation of liberty." It seems entirely possible that Amalickiah was not aiming to lead a few people out of the church of God in an effort to create passive theological dissenters. He led away their hearts so that they would become like him. His goal was to create people who would advocate wickedness and persuade even more people to destroy the church and to destroy liberty.

Readers are left to consider a disturbing parallel potentiality: if Alma's great wickedness was using

was "going about to destroy the church of God" *Mosiah 27:10*	"causing much dissension among the people" *Mosiah 27:9*	"blessed the earth for righteous' sake...For this is the cursing and the blessing of God upon the land" *Alma 45:16*
tries "to destroy the church of God *Alma 46:10*	"they were led away by Amalickiah to dissensions" *Alma 46:6*	"...blessing God had sent upon the face of the land for the righteous' sake" *Alma 46:10*

FIGURE 4 Alma and Amalickiah comparison

flattery to convince many people to "do after the manner of his iniquities"—and Mosiah 27:8 says it was—then it is entirely possible that Alma "murdered many of [God's] children" by convincing them to do exactly what he did: reject Christ, dissent from the church, and be numbered among the unbelievers in both belief and practice (Alma 36:14). The end result of Alma leading many to do what he did is not necessarily a group of quiet unbelievers but a generation of vocal and aggressive dissenters.

It may be merely a highly ironic coincidence that the years Alma spends as chief judge and as high priest are rife with Nephite hostility. Perhaps it is a sad fluke that, except for Sherem, the Book of Mormon's dissenters "all arose during the late monarchal period and the early reign of the judges."[6] What is indisputable is that Alma spends the last nineteen years of his life facing a steady stream of apostates and anti-Christs and coping with dissenter-provoked, dissenter-led, and dissenter-supported battles. The question is why all of the dissenters arrive in the first few decades of the reign of the judges while Alma is the political and ecclesiastical leader. The answer very possibly is Alma, himself. Prior to his conversion, Alma persuaded and persecuted; he convinced and possibly created the generation of aggressive anti-Christs, duplicitous dissenters, and half-hearted, faltering believers that he spent the last two decades of his life trying to reclaim.

righteous man

Prior to the angel's rebuke, Alma's life story is derived from general labels, understated hints, parallel structure, and interpretation. Nevertheless, one aspect of Alma is certain: Alma was a very wicked man. Some readers may reject this interpretation, fearing that Alma's past will challenge them, arguing that it lacks conclusive evidence. That is true—but before readers discard Alma's unbeliever past, the possibility that his chance to destroy the church of God was over, and his comparability with Amalickiah, they should consider whether the misguided, youthful image is more justified. Alma's story can be read that way, and it is certainly more comfortable, but is it supported by more evidence? It may feel profoundly disturbing to interpret preconversion Alma as a wicked, idolatrous, unbelieving, adult anti-Christ, but there are many reasons to believe that he was—and that is not only good news, it is critical.

Readers know Alma was converted sometime in the turbulent century before Christ came. He changed utterly and completely, and that is a hopeful story, no matter Alma's age or wickedness. But it is a more hopeful story if Alma was "redeemed from the gall of bitterness and bonds of iniquity" (Mosiah 27:29). Understanding who preconversion Alma was is not for the fainthearted; it is for the brokenhearted. The story of this idolatrous man is not necessarily needed for the hopeful, but it is desperately needed for the hopeless. The point is not to vilify, but to testify: understanding the depths of Alma's wickedness is understanding the depths to which Christ willingly descends to rescue. Believing that someone like Alma can find the marvelous light of God means believing that change is challenging, but repentance is real. The past may be stubborn, but conversion transforms, even if others do not see it, even if one is a wild teenager, a middle-aged unbeliever, a reformed unbeliever, or a fallible leader of others. Understanding Alma means knowing that even those who have "[lived] without God in the world" can cry out to the Redeemer they rejected and find him (Mosiah 27:31). Understanding Alma means allowing that your very wicked self and your very wicked neighbors can be redeemed. It means being born again.

And then it means choosing to grow up. Alma is not a stereotype, and he is not paragon. He was a regular man who became very wicked, chose to be an unbeliever, and found himself in the darkest abyss. But that makes his story even better—because in that abyss he chose hope. He chose a new story. And then it began.

3

This We Know, That He Was a Righteous Man

Alma disappears from the Book of Mormon in Alma 45:18. The next verse is a poetic eulogy, probably written by Alma's son, Helaman, though it is an odd one. Five different unsure declarations and hesitant suppositions close with the firm—and apparently unironic—statement: "We know nothing concerning [Alma's] death and burial" (Alma 45:19). Only one phrase stands out for affirming what is known: "This we know, that he was a righteous man" (verse 19). This lone statement of positive knowledge draws attention but only provokes more questions. Instead of stating Alma's status as a simple fact ("Alma was a righteous man"), the author adds a subject who knows this fact ("This we know…"). Readers may wonder who this "we" is. Who knows Alma was righteous? And if "we" think he is righteous, are others skeptical? Conflicted? Oppositional?

That some members of his society may doubt Alma's sincerity seems realistic. That modern readers are surprised by that doubt that develops at least in part because a myopic focus on Alma's righteousness is built into the structure of his story. If a modern family reads one chapter per day, they read of Alma's unbeliever days for a single day, and then they spend a month and a half on the forty-five chapters and over one hundred pages of Alma's righteous era. Technically, this covers a mere nineteen chronological years, but the expanse of narrative time (and physical space) given to Alma's righteousness can lull readers into nearly forgetting preconversion Alma's wickedness.[1] Readers naturally minimize Alma's past to near nonexistence, but they must remember Alma's former wickedness to make sense of stories and statements such as the one in Alma 45 about his disappearance. Reading Alma as an anti-Christ on par with Nehor and Korihor reframes Alma's ministry, clarifies his interpersonal relationships, and distills his theological preoccupations. Knowledge of Alma's unbelieving past changes perspectives and interpretations of events and relationships, and it offers deep and tragic insight into his emotional and psychological state. Without this perspective, Alma's stories are perplexing.

The backdrop of Alma's past clarifies episodes during his reign as chief judge. Nehor, for example, arrives in Alma's first year as chief judge, establishes a church, gains a following, then suddenly whips out a sword during a religious street debate and kills the elderly Gideon (Alma 1:9). The murder is shocking, irrational, and violent, especially because it takes place in front of an audience of church members (verse 7). When they bring him to Alma, Nehor rashly "plead[s] for himself with much boldness" (verse 11). It hardly seems possible that someone as involved in the community as Nehor could be unaware that killing Gideon is a crime for which he could be condemned. The people recently acknowledged the laws and the new system of government and were therefore "obliged to abide" these laws (verse 1). Nehor's boldness is bizarre, even perilous. Wearing costly apparel is a much more minor expression of the same inexplicable behavior. There is no law against fancy clothing, but it appears in the Book of Mormon only as a symptom of pride, arrogance, and vanity. Why would Nehor wear "very costly apparel" (verse 6) when members of the church believe in wearing "neat and comely" apparel (verse 27)? Such a display of vanity is hardly helpful in persuading the chief judge that he is innocent of a capital crime that multiple people witnessed. The story is confusing because Nehor's motivations are mystifying.

However, the encounter looks different if we remember that Alma likely dressed and spoke like Nehor only a few years earlier. Nehor appears in the first year of the reign of the judges (Alma 1:2), but that does not mean that he arrives in Zarahemla, hears what is being discussed, chooses his doctrine, gains a following, convinces his followers to support him in style, and establishes a church in less than a year (while still leaving enough time to debate, kill Gideon, have his trial, be condemned, and suffer an ignominious death). As others have noted, it seems more likely that Nehor was interacting with and preaching to the people of Zarahemla before Alma became the first chief judge.[2] Nehor's ideas resemble unbeliever preaching, most notably the proposition that "every priest and teacher...ought not to labor with their hands" (belief 6) but "ought to be supported by the people" (belief 5) (Alma 1:3). Nehor believes that "all mankind should be saved," which correlates with the unbelievers' refusal to call upon God and repent (belief 4), and if his altercation with Gideon is any indication, he believes violence is justified (belief 7).

When Nehor "stood before Alma and [plead] for himself with much boldness," he seems reckless about his very life (Alma 1:11). However, that same attitude may be credulity if Nehor is a preacher of unbeliever-based doctrine and finds himself being judged by a former unbeliever. Nehor's boldness may be the brash assumption that Alma has not really changed or that a changed Alma can be bullied and humiliated by the reminder of his past. How far will Alma go in enforcing the laws he violated when he and the sons of Mosiah were working "contrary to the commandments of God, or even the king" (Mosiah 27:10)?

Will a former unbeliever actually sentence Nehor to death? Though Alma names Nehor's crime as priest-craft and lawfully condemns Nehor for "enforc[ing] it by the sword" (Alma 1:12), Nehor never repents. He maintains his disdain to the bitter end, even when he is "caused, or rather did acknowledge" his mistake (verse 15). Notably, the mistake that Nehor is caused to confess is not the crime for which he was condemned (killing Gideon) but, rather, for preaching "contrary to the word of God" (verse 15). Nehor is a hotheaded, conceited killer, but he is not unfathomable. His bold-ness, his arrogance, and his refusal to repent or apol-ogize are understandable—he is sentenced to die by a former unbeliever, someone who persecuted others and broke the law of Mosiah, too.

This encounter with Nehor parallels Alma's con-version speech: both demonstrate the impact of Alma's unbelieving past. Though readers may forget Alma's dissent when they close the book of Mosiah, turning the page does not mean everyone in the story forgets. Nehor preached unbeliever ideas, and his followers who withdraw do as well. These dissenters persecute many (belief 7). They persecute church members who believe in Christ (Alma 1:19), humble church members who do not indulge in wearing costly apparel (Alma 1:32), and priests and teachers who do not charge money for imparting the word of God (beliefs 2, 5, and 6) (Alma 1:20). As the high priest of the church, Alma is upset when those who follow Nehor "with[draw] them-selves" from the church (Alma 1:24)—and for good cause. Moreover, this is merely the first in a long line of dissenters and anti-Christs whose beliefs align to some degree with Alma's preconversion beliefs.

Amlici arrives a few years later with a firm "intent to destroy the church of God" (Alma 2:4) and becomes the Nephite king (Alma 2:2). He has a different plan and approach, but he is "after the order of the man that slew Gideon by the sword" (verse 1). Similar to Nehor, it is inconceivable that Amlici could arrive, gain a following, provoke an election about kingship, and start a civil war while secretly creating an alliance with the Lamanites. He must also have the Lamanites join that war, lose, and then start another Nephite-Lamanite war—all occurring during the fifth year of the reign of the judges.

In the first war, Alma and Amlici battle face-to-face and "contend mightily, one with another" (verse 29). Alma pleads to God to spare him, that he may be "an instrument in [God's] hands to save and preserve this people" (verse 30), and then he finds himself strengthened enough to "[slay] Amlici with the sword" (verse 31). If they knew each other previously or even if they both believed unbeliever doctrine, this moment is fraught with psychological tension (Alma 4:1).

Tensions flare again in the ninth year of the reign of the judges when church members apostatize to the point that they lead the "unbelievers on from one piece of iniquity to another" (Alma 4:11), an ironic role reversal; this time it is the church members who persecute the "needy and the naked" and the "sick and afflicted" (verse 12). Some members remain humble and maintain their belief in the resurrection of the dead (belief 3) and deliverance through Jesus Christ (belief 4), but these people have persecutions "heaped upon them by the remainder of his people" (belief 7) (Alma 4:15). Seeing the resulting inequality (belief 5) causes Alma to be very sorrowful—so sorrowful that the narrator hastens to reassure readers that "the Spirit of the Lord did not fail" Alma (verse 15). The additional explanatory clause seems strange. Why does the narrator (Mormon) assume that the Spirit might fail the high priest of the church of God? Or is the narrator quoting Alma? The phrase is unique. No one else in the Book of Mormon is worried about the Spirit of the Lord failing, ever. Only when readers recall that Alma has unique reasons to think the Spirit of the Lord might fail him does this make sense.

Eventually Alma resigns as chief judge to "[confine] himself wholly to the high priesthood" and preach "the testimony of the word" of God (Alma 4:20). For the next ten years, Alma is engaged in missionary work, telling his people to "Repent...for the kingdom of heaven is nigh at hand" (Alma 9:25). Speaking in Gideon may be the only truly happy interaction Alma records after his conversion. Even preaching there is tainted with oblique references to the Amlicite/Lamanite war (Alma 7:1) and not-so-oblique references to the "state of so much unbelief" that Alma found in Zarahemla (Alma 7:6). In one lengthy sentence, Alma details the problems he saw in Zarahemla while praising the people in Gideon: the citizens of Gideon are "not lifted up in the pride of [their] hearts"; "have not set [their] hearts upon riches and the vain things of the world"; and "do not worship idols," but do "look forward for the remission of [their] sins, with an everlasting faith, which is to come" (Alma 7:6). Alma works with, preaches to, and judges people who are dwindling in unbelief, people who hold to at least two or three—and sometimes many more—of the ideas that concerned the unbelievers.

When readers view Alma as the very wicked and idolatrous unbeliever that the narrator describes, they likely interpret the text differently. Even though the setting, the characters, the dialogue, the plot, and every single word is the same, Alma's toughest moments as a missionary are burdened with heart-wrenching poignancy. As an unbeliever, he "[stole] away the hearts of the people" and "caused much dissension among the people" (Mosiah 27:9). From that perspective, readers witness Alma reaching out to the unbelievers and those who are dwindling in unbelief, "zealously striving to repair all the injuries" he caused by "exhorting [the people] with long-suffering and much travail to keep the commandments of God" (Mosiah 27:35, 33).

The events at Ammonihah have the most dramatically different tone and message. Though Alma "[begins] to preach" (Alma 8:8), the Book of Mormon does not record any of these words. The first recorded words of this one-sided dialogue are the people announcing, *"we know that thou art* Alma; and *we know that thou art* high priest over the church which thou hast established...according to your tradition" (verse 11; my emphasis). The parallel phrasing is a poetic device and signals to readers that something important is happening. If this is an introduction, then the Ammonihahites introduce themselves by saying they know who Alma is and then pointedly not acknowledging Alma's service as chief judge.

Echoing the first set of parallel "we know that thou art" statements, the people then assert who they are not: *"and we are not* of thy church, and *we do not* believe in such foolish traditions" (Alma 8:11; my emphasis). The words are not only rude but also accusatory: the people claim that Alma established a church. Referring to it as *thy church* rather than the church of God is not a random pronoun but a subtle allegation of priestcraft (establishing one's own church for money or power). They then link Alma's church with foolish traditions. A conversation between Aaron and an Amalekite dissenter during the same time period clarifies that *foolish traditions* refers to the forefathers' belief that one can know of things to come, particularly Christ and resurrection for the dead (see Alma 21:7–9). Considering their further discussions, it is likely that Ammonihahites use the term similarly. The people make two more assertions of knowledge and then break the pattern with one direct statement of fact: "Therefore, thou art not the chief judge over us" (Alma

8:12). The people "spit upon [Alma]" and cast him out of the city (Alma 8:13).

The argument is short, but it is too well-stated and too parallel to be random. Instead of momentary annoyance, this is directed hostility. The narrator later discloses a connection between the people in Ammonihah and Nehor (Alma 14:16), which suggests the people may be motivated by resentment about Alma's condemnation of Nehor. But the people never mention Nehor, his death, his order, or his faith. Their aggression is focused on Alma, his church, and his foolish traditions. They know who Alma is, they remind him he has no legal power, they do not recognize any priestly authority, and they could accuse him of a crime. Their message is clear, and Alma understands. When the people throw him out, Alma does not fight to stay. He departs and begins walking to the city of Aaron (Alma 8:13).

At this point, readers may imagine Alma as scared or angry, but he is "weighed down with much sorrow" and "wading through much tribulation and anguish of soul" (Alma 8:14). The phrasing evokes Alma's own repentance, his process of "wading through much tribulation" (Mosiah 27:28) and being in "the most bitter pain and anguish of soul" (Alma 38:8). It seems that something about this interaction triggers memories of his own unbelieving past and his repentance. He may be thinking generally of sin and the universal need for repentance and reconciliation through Christ—or he may be thinking of Ammonihah, unbelievers, and who he was before the first year of the reign of the judges. Alma was numbered among the unbelievers, and the people in Ammonihah are aligning themselves with the ideas of those unbelievers. The narrator says the people in Ammonihah are Nehorite. If so, then Nehor had unstated beliefs that align almost perfectly with unbelievers. If not, then both Nehor and the people in

Ammonihah have theological roots in the unbeliever movement (see FIGURE 5, next page).

Ultimately, the horrifying and tragic reality is that the people in Ammonihah—just like Nehor, Amlici, and so many others—teach philosophies that resemble the contentions held to be true by the unbelievers. Nehor starts a church, Amlici starts a war, and the people in Ammonihah light a fire and then throw in scriptures, women, and children. They choose to kill innocent people in a torturous way and to force Alma and Amulek to watch. Even if Alma is the worst of the unbelievers, the man who betrayed their cause, condemned a fellow unbeliever, and now walks around the countryside preaching his new Christian faith—even if all that is true, the Ammonihahite actions are unjustifiable. That Alma walked away from this city the first time with memories of crying out to God for mercy and wading through strong emotion is not surprising. He walked away knowing that the people in Ammonihah question the same doctrines that the unbelievers questioned over a decade ago. He has condemned Nehor, fought with Amlici, preached at Zarahemla, and pleaded with Ammonihah's angry people. But they still light their horrific fires and burn all those who trade unbelief for belief. When Alma walks away from Ammonihah the second time, the Book of Mormon does not describe how he feels. If Alma had perished in Ammonihah, his story would be utterly sad, but he would have been spared the emotional trauma of surviving.

Nevertheless, Alma has not completed his mission; he must encounter more anti-Christs and people whose beliefs or practices resemble those of the unbelievers. Korihor instigates another movement toward dissension in the seventeenth year of the reign of the judges (Alma 30); after that, the Zoramites explicitly reject "the tradition of our brethren" and the "childishness of

Unbelievers	Ammonihah	Nehor
Do not believe the traditions of their fathers	Alma 8:11; Alma 9:8	
Do not believe concerning the coming of Christ	Alma 11:32–33 (26–42)	
Do not believe what has been said concerning the resurrection of the dead	Alma 11:42; Alma 12:8, 21	
Do not believe in calling upon the Lord their God	Alma 13:28	Alma 1:4
Do not believe that there should be an equality among all men		Alma 1:3
Do not believe that all their priests and teachers should labor with their own hands for their support		Alma 1:3
Do believe in persecution, especially if the object of persecution is members of the Church of God	Alma 8:13; Alma 14:7, 8, 17–25	Alma 1:7,9
Do believe in proselytizing, especially with "flattering words"	Alma 10:15; Alma 12:3–4	

FIGURE 5 Unbeliever influence

their fathers" (belief 1), insisting that "there shall be no Christ" (belief 2) (Alma 31:16). Ultimately, Alma's own son Corianton struggles with doctrines that sound extraordinarily similar to the doctrines of the unbelievers, namely problems "concerning the coming of Christ," especially doubt about how and "why these things should be known so long beforehand" (belief 2) (Alma 39:15, 17); worries "concerning the resurrection for the dead" (belief 3) (Alma 40:1, see also Alma 40); a question about whether he needs to repent for his sins (belief 4) (Alma 39:3–9); and a desire for riches, possibly wanting to acquire the "vain things of this world" without laboring with his own hands to get them (belief 6) (Alma 39:14).

Alma's conversion frames the opening (and closing) of a story about a brilliant rhetorician, strong chief judge, and dedicated disciple of Christ. It has often been read as a coming-of-age narrative, the story of a stereotypical rebellious teenager becoming a mature church leader—but Alma's transformation may be much more dramatic. He may be a skilled anti-Christ who repents so profoundly and embraces Christ and forgiveness so fully that he becomes the leader of the church of God. Nevertheless, Alma's personal reformation does not erase the consequences of his former actions. His nineteen-year record is about his people and their struggles, but it is also about the man who is watching his people as they leave the church of God, instigate civil war, dissent to the Lamanites, and instigate more war—typically over theological issues that bear strong resemblances to his prior beliefs. Alma documents one demoralizing encounter after another; his rescue missions become more personal, more tense, more psychologically complex, and much more emotionally devastating. They culminate with Alma answering his own unbelieving questions, now posed by his youngest son, Corianton. Alma finally has answers; he has spent the years since his conversion "inquir[ing] diligently of God that [he] might know" God's answers to the same questions that personally worried him (Alma 40:3).

This is the narrative of a deeply repentant man who is "zealously striving to repair all the injuries" he has "done to the church" (Mosiah 27:35), and who is hopeful at the beginning that he can do so. When persecutors do not repent, he and other church members suffer under this trial (Alma 1:23). As people continue not to repent, church members feel great sorrow (Alma 4:7), and Alma becomes very sorrowful, so much so that there is concern that the Spirit of the Lord might fail him (Alma 4:15). After joy in Gideon (Alma 7:5), Alma is "weighed down with sorrow" at Ammonihah (Alma 8:14), feeling "great anxiety even unto pain" (Alma 13:27). He rejoices to find that the sons of Mosiah have remained faithful for fourteen years, perhaps because of the great sorrow he feels when learning yet again of iniquity among his people (Alma 31:2). Alma's sorrow initially appears to be the sorrow of a prophet yearning for his people to be righteous, but that sorrow increases. Eventually his sorrow is so exceeding that it manifests as physical pain (Alma 31:24, 30, 31). Nephi's brother Jacob explains that high priests of God agree to "[answer] the sins of the people upon our own heads if we did not teach them the word of God with all diligence" (Jacob 1:19). Alma may have the weight of an extra burden. He has the sorrow of his people's poor choices. He also has the deeper sorrow that the beliefs he formerly preached have become deeply rooted in Nephite communities and have led multitudes astray and away from Christ.

Alma knows he was an unbeliever. He knows he repented and was born again in Christ. Reformed, Alma devotes his life to rescuing unbelievers, but he discovers that most do not want to be rescued, at least not by him. Greatly persecuted and smitten from nearly the first moment of his conversion, he learns hard truths: he can change, but others may not. God may forgive, but others may not. Alma's narrative is powerful, but painful; it is disconcerting, but realistic. Shrinking Alma's dangerous theological dissension into a teen-aged-sized stereotype may feel safe, but this interpretation has a price: it reduces Alma's need for the grace of Jesus Christ, it diminishes the depth of Alma's repentance, and it simplifies Alma's comprehension of the magnitude of Christ's atonement—the very doctrines that define Alma's most powerful sermons.

From Alma's words, readers learn that the Savior is "mighty to save and to cleanse from all unrighteousness" (Alma 7:14), and from his life story, readers understand that God can and will save unbelievers, idolaters, persecutors, flatterers, and dissenters. He saves those who burned in the fire, and he can save those who burned them, if they will accept him and the grace he offers. Because Alma was personally transformed by Christ, he can explain why sinfulness might require "repenting nigh unto death" (Mosiah 27:28) and why angelic visits do not preempt the process: inquiring diligently and fasting and praying many days is required if one wants to know these things of oneself (Alma 5:46). The doctrine of Christ is precious regardless of who teaches it, but when Alma witnesses that the Savior's "bowels may be filled with mercy" for him or for anyone, readers should be thinking of a very wicked man who led many people astray (Alma 7:12). When they read that the Savior suffers "pains and afflictions and temptations of every kind" so that he may know perfectly "how to succor his people according to their infirmities," readers should think about Alma, sorry and sorrowful, depressed yet driven, preaching the gospel for decades to people who still believe the doctrines he mistakenly taught them years before (Alma 7:11–12). Retelling his story is the way to end his story, and it circumscribes his righteous life and leaves each of his three sons with the messages he thought were most critical for them to know.

Inspired by their father, Alma's sons immediately "go forth among the people, to declare the word unto them" (Alma 43:1). Knowing what he knows of his past and living what he is living in his present compels Alma to join them: "Alma, also, himself, *could not* rest, and he also went forth" (Alma 43:1; my emphasis). The sentence is elusive but significant. It may be a tragic commentary on people's inability to forgive and the heavy burden of being unable to fix the past—or the exact opposite: a statement of triumph about the grace of God, the joy of redemption, and the desire for everyone to hear the good news. It can be read either way, but it must be read in one critical way: whether Alma's inability to rest is a tragedy or a triumph, it is the choice and action of a righteous man.

PART II

Chapters 4–6

Joseph Spencer's "The Structure of the Book of Alma" insightfully argues that the book of Alma is holistically structured. Broken into halves (Alma 1–29 and Alma 30–63), which are then halved again (Alma 1–16, 17–29 and Alma 30–44, 45–63) leaves quarter-sized sections: Alma 1–16 parallels Alma 30–44, and Alma 17–29 parallels Alma 45–63. One brief example demonstrates the powerful argument: Alma's three missionary journeys (Zarahemla, Gideon, Ammonihah) align with Alma's three speeches to his sons (Helaman, Shiblon, Corianton) in length, approach, audience concerns, and even audience righteousness. Fortunately, audience reaction differs; despite similar unbeliever philosophies, Corianton responds better than the Ammonihahites to Alma's lengthiest message. Dozens of articles and books have been written about Alma's stories and speeches and also about the sons of Mosiah and their fourteen-year missionary journey, but many skip the concluding sections as simple narrative "aftermath and cleanup," rather than doctrine.

Alma 27–29, original chapter XV, is easily overlooked, though it ought not to be. Neglecting these chapters may leave readers believing that the sons of Mosiah's mission concludes with success (partially) and peace (not at all), or that Alma's "Oh that I were an angel" speech is missionary-themed poetry (unlikely) motivated by his joy over the sons of Mosiah's return (minimally) and perhaps a hint of envy (almost impossible). Alma 27–29 does highlight the sons of Mosiah and their mission's aftermath, but like Alma's mission, it concludes with some success and pervasive pain. The aftermath of the Lamanite mission is death and destruction, unifying it thematically with the conclusion of Alma's tragic mission to Ammonihah.

This neglected section is the focus of the following chapters. Chapter 4 analyzes the Nephite conception of mourning, finding a complex and intricate practice rather than a simplistic, artificial separation between faithful sadness and unfaithful devastation. Chapter 5 explores assumptions about Alma 29. The historical context of widespread grief and mourning hint that the chapter may not be missionary-themed. Chapter 6 contemplates the formal structure of Alma 29, not to classify the chapter based on technicalities, but to uncover practical ways that the emotionally damaged, possibly traumatized author found healing and hope in writing a personal psalm of lament modeled on Nephi's structure.

These chapters both correspond to and yet reverse the first half of this book. Both sections study how understanding particular moments alter interpretations of other moments. Examining Alma's sinfulness (Mosiah 27) changes how we read his encounters in his future (Alma 1–29). Similarly, but from the opposite direction, examining community and personal woundedness in Alma 27–29 changes how we read the past (Alma 1–26). In a sense, both the past and the future overlap in the present, and they do so in pinnacle of grievous harm. Nevertheless, Alma 29 demonstrates a healing and hopeful practice.

4

The Cry of Mourning Was Heard

At baptism, members of The Church of Jesus Christ of Latter-day Saints indicate that they are "willing to mourn with those who mourn" (Mosiah 18:9), a doctrine that may not always harmonize fully with practice. Scriptures such as 2 Nephi 9:6 teach that death will "[pass] upon all" as part of "the merciful plan of the great Creator," and Alma 42:8 explains that a world without death "would destroy the great plan of happiness." These doctrines and others, such as the belief that families can maintain eternal relationships after death, comfort modern Church members. Many assume that faith in such consoling doctrine will minimize or even eclipse grief. If personal losses create deep pain and long-lasting grief, Church members may wonder if their faith is failing.[1] As a non–Latter-day Saint scholar explains, sometimes Latter-day Saint doctrine can unintentionally "stigmatize grief and bereavement, as though these emotional responses were indications of character weakness or lack of faith."[2] Grief can be compounded with worry and guilt as members conclude that they ought not to feel the sorrow they are feeling.

The conflicting impulses between faith and mourning that confuse members of the Church today are evident in Book of Mormon narratives, though less than members of the modern Church might expect. Mourning begins with Nephi questioning Sariah's sorrow for her sons (1 Ne. 5:1) and does not end until Mormon fears that his words will "grieve thee, to weigh thee down unto death" (Moro. 9:25). Mourning permeates the Book of Mormon. The phrasing that describes Ether's hopelessness (Ether 15:34), the people's response to "death and destruction" (Alma 28:14), and Jacob's reaction to "wickedness and abominations" (Jacob 2:31) assumes that mourning is natural. While readers may recall the widespread mourning in the closing scenes of the Book of Mormon, the people living in the years before Christ comes are also acquainted with sorrow. Alma 28 refers to mourning more than any other chapter and contextualizes that mourning within a story. The author portrays Nephite traditions and practices regarding death, destruction, and mourning, leaving behind stories that explain who mourns, how they mourn, and why some mourn more than others. What is described in scripture complicates a simplistic assumption of faithful sadness or unfaithful devastation, drawing attention to a realistic portrayal of loss as well as a more nuanced theology of grief.

Mourning first appears in the Book of Mormon when Sariah mourns her sons and then when the daughters of Ishmael mourn their father, stories that the first volume of this series analyzes from a gender-relations perspective.[3] Sariah, thinking her sons had died in the wilderness, "truly had mourned because of [them]" (1 Ne. 5:1). This description is straightforward, but the following sentences connect Sariah's mourning to fear, and fear to "complaining," twice noting that Sariah "complained against" Lehi for being a "visionary man" (1 Ne. 5:2, 3). Nephi may not be quoting word for word a conversation that he did not hear and is writing about years later, but the way he writes makes it seem as if he is. Sariah admits her mistake, saying, "Now I know of a surety that the Lord hath commanded my husband...[and] hath protected my sons" (1 Ne. 5:8). Although the encounter may tell readers more about Nephi and his assumptions than about Sariah, readers can skim the story and walk away believing that mothers with faith do not mourn.

The daughters of Ishmael mourn next. Nephi summarizes that the daughters "mourn exceedingly because of the loss of their father, and because of their afflictions in the wilderness; and they did murmur against my father" (1 Ne. 16:35). The sentence slips easily from mourning to murmuring and labels the women as "daughters of Ishmael," despite their recent marriages to Nephi and his brothers (1 Ne. 16:35). Nephi again seems to quote. The daughters of Ishmael say, "Our father is dead; yea, and we have wandered much in the wilderness, and we have suffered much...and after all these sufferings we must perish" (1 Ne. 16:35). Nephi notes both beforehand and afterward that the words are "murmuring against my father" (1 Ne. 16:35, 36). Additionally, he informs the reader that the murmuring was "also against me" (1 Ne. 16:36). If the daughters are insinuating that Ishmael's death is directly related to the lack of food in the wilderness, Nephi may be feeling defensive because of his recent broken bow. Alternatively, perhaps he simply is not as empathetic as he should be—and seems to become after Lehi dies, an experience that draws extraordinary emotion and pain (2 Ne. 4). Yet with so few direct quotations of women's words in the Book of Mormon, these words that he labels as "murmuring" are disproportionately loud.

How much these two incidents contribute to the stigmatization of mourning is difficult to measure. The impact may be exaggerated in the minds of modern readers, who likely equate Sariah's complaints with "fault finding." Yet complaints can be simple expressions of grief or lament, according to Webster's 1828 dictionary. However, even in 1828, to complain *against* someone had a more negative connotation, one not unlike someone who murmurs, or "utter[s] complaints in a low voice" or "utter[s] sullen discontent."[4] Despite

Nephi's equating of the words, neither murmuring nor complaining against someone has much to do with mourning, which technically is "the act of sorrowing or expressing grief."[5] But because readers first encounter mourning through these tense moments of gender conflict, because Nephi seems to quote mourning women as if they were whining, and because Sariah admits her misjudgment, the first book of the Book of Mormon seems to connect mourning, distrust, and weakness, and then ties these traits to female grumbling and a need for repentance, creating doubt and distrust about a natural process.

Although Nephi seems critical of people mourning, the universality of mourning is evident in Alma 28 when "great mourning and lamentation" is heard "among all the people of Nephi," apparently loud enough that it can be "heard throughout all the land" (Alma 28:4):

> And now this was a time that there was a great
> *mourning and lamentation heard* throughout
>   all the land,
> *among all the people of Nephi* (Alma 28:4;
>   my emphasis).
>
> Yea, the cry of widows mourning for
>   their husbands,
> And also of fathers mourning for their sons,
> And the daughter for the brother,
> Yea, the brother for the father;
>
> and thus the cry of
> *mourning was heard*
> *among all of them* (Alma 28:5; my emphasis).

These verses hide an *inclusio*, a poetic technique that places a set of ideas or words at the beginning and ending of a section in a manner that frames the interior section. The first statement—"a great mourning and lamentation heard throughout all the land, among all the people"—is echoed in abbreviated but clearly parallel language one verse later. The key ideas are emphasized by the repetition: "mourning" being "heard" "among all."

The cries of mourning in Alma 28 are most likely audible. The repetitious wording of the inclusio describes the mourning as something "heard throughout all the land, among all the people (verse 4) and repeats at the end that the "mourning was heard among all of them" (verse 5). Mourning and lamentation are regularly described as a cry, and a few stories confirm the audible range of that cry. For example, when Nephi, the son of Helaman, laments over wickedness on his tower in his private garden, he is overheard by people walking by on the highway (Hel. 7:10). The Lamanite prophet, Samuel, not only prophesies to the Nephites that they will "cry unto the Lord" but also affirms the audible range when he says that the people will "weep and howl" (Hel. 13:32). Unlike inaudible weeping in many modern cultures, Book of Mormon lamenting or weeping was vocalized, perhaps similar to biblical laments, which ranged from "loud...howling and screaming" to "light whimpering."[6]

The inclusio in Alma 28 frames a list of people who are mourning for loved ones. Notably, the people are all named by family relationship. The Bible[7] and the Book of Mormon both rely on the technique of listing individual mourners to symbolically represent the totality of society, but where the Bible might list people by occupation or age or some other defining characteristic, the Book of Mormon consistently lists mourners by family relationship, almost as if they are defined by that relationship. Moroni speaks of the widows and orphans who will mourn in the last days because their husbands or fathers are dead (Mormon 8:40). Mormon lists the most inclusive family in the Book of Mormon: sons, daughters, fathers, mothers, husbands, and wives (Mormon 6:19). This list highlights the deep tragedy of the Book of Mormon: Mormon alone laments every member of a family and names them by their familial relationships, but he does so when every Nephite family is lost. All of these people are dead (Mormon 6:18–19).

Alma 28:5 is noticeably not a complete listing. The list is lopsided: there are widows mourning husbands, but no mothers mourning their sons; daughters mourn for brothers, but no daughters mourn for fathers; and brothers mourn for fathers, but not for other brothers. This lopsidedness makes sense if readers realize every single *individual* in the family is represented—widows (mothers), fathers, daughters, and brothers (sons) (see FIGURE 6). Moreover, each individual suffers when his or her male relatives—husbands, sons, brothers, and fathers—are killed in the war. Ultimately, this poem makes most sense when the people are recognized both individually and relationally. These people are named by their family relationships (the young woman in the poem is a "daughter," not a "girl"), yet the poem only balances when that girl is seen as one member of a nuclear family (this daughter suffers for her personal loss, not a generalized family loss) (see FIGURE 6).

Grieving, each individual "cries" for his or her loss (Alma 28:5). The description of who is lamenting about whom demonstrates poetic *catabasis*, a literary technique in which each successive descending line maintains obvious parallelism, while diminishing in length.

The lines literally shrink in words, creating a feeling of slowly dwindling and, when written poetically, visually depict that waning. The words seem to wither under the weight of loss and grief, as if the poet who

Members of family who mourn
Yea, the cry of widows mourning for their husbands,
And also of fathers mourning for their sons,
And the daughter for the brother,
Yea, the brother for the father;

Male family members killed in war
Yea, the cry of widows mourning for their husbands,
And also of fathers mourning for their sons,
And the daughter for the brother,
Yea, the brother for the father;

Mourners in relationship
Yea, the cry of [wives] mourning for their husbands,
And also of [fathers] mourning for their sons,
And the [sisters] for the brother,
Yea, the [sons] for the father;

FIGURE 6 Alma 28:5 Relationships

hears the cries is weighed down with the pain and can barely write the words.

The interior of the poetic inclusio in Alma 28:4–5 may reveal even more information about Nephite family life, revealing why some have reason to mourn more. Although every mourner is named by whom he or she is within a specific family relationship, the mourners are not all listed as mourning the relationship that named them (see FIGURE 6). For example, the brother, the last mourner in the poem, is mourning for his father, even though one would expect a brother to mourn his brother, and a son to mourn his father. The daughter in the poem is mourning her brother. Why is she not a sister mourning her brother? Notably, the first line tells readers that widows are mourning for their husbands. Why are wives not mourning for their husbands? This may merely be the awkwardness forced on the poem so that the family relationships could be listed, but it appears to be something more: the family seems renamed by loss. When a young girl's brother dies, she is no longer called sister; the poem labels her as daughter. Likewise, when a young man's father passes away, he loses the title of "son" and is left to be named by another relationship: brother. A wife is no longer a wife when her husband is gone. She is now a widow. When this mother and children lose male family members in a war, they are no longer called by the name or title that identifies that relationship. When husbands are dead, wives become "widows." When fathers are dead, sons become "brothers." When brothers are dead, sisters become "daughters." There is only one exception: the father. The father in this poem is mourning for his son. Unlike every other person in the family, when a father loses his son, he is still called father. This is unfortunately suggestive of the place of women and children in Nephite society; they may be named only in relation to the living males in their lives.

It is not only death poetry in Alma 28 that suggests that Nephite[8] women and children carry an extra burden when a husband/father passes away. A similar poetic listing is found in Mosiah 21, which does not rename women and children by their loss, but does clarify a terrifying reality facing a widow with young children. In this poem, there is a noticeable absence of fathers and husbands mourning among Limhi's battle-worn people, likely because so many had been killed:

> And now there was a great mourning and
>   lamentation among the people of Limhi,
> The widow mourning for her husband,
> The son and the daughter mourning
>   for their father,
> And the brothers for their brethren (verse 9).

This war left a "great many widows...[who] cry mightily from day to day," fearing another war with the Lamanites (Mosiah 21:10). King Limhi commands the remaining men to "impart to the support of the widows and their children, that they might not perish with hunger" (verse 17), and the society gathers "together in a body" for that purpose (verse 18). The Book of Mormon cites biblical law specifically concerning the treatment of widows and orphans. Within biblical tradition, a widow not only did not inherit her husband's property but she herself was "passed into the power" of the heir of her husband.[9] Even though those who neglected their duties to the fatherless and the widows are condemned in the strongest of terms (see Ex. 22:22–24), the situation for an adult woman was precarious, and a widow with minor children was vulnerable to extreme poverty.

The remainder of Limhi's people gather, and thereafter the community is spoken of as a unit, except when Gideon refers once to "our women and children" and the narrator comments about "their women and children" (Mosiah 22:8, 2). Both references are in lists of property. While modern readers may bristle over the possessive pronoun and intimation that women and children were property, it has precedent in biblical law, and a widow facing starvation might have been relieved to be one of the group. These widows grieve, but their "cry of mourning" may also be a cry of fear. If Nephites follow biblical traditions and laws about property rights and inheritance, then the family who loses a father/husband faces not only death but also destitution, even starvation.

More than forty verses in the Book of Mormon refer to mourning, the majority of which are in narrative sections and refer to stories of individuals mourning the deaths of loved ones. A substantial portion, however, are in persuasive embedded documents that would

Mourning and Endless Wo
Alma 28:11
many thousands are mourning
for the loss of their kindred,
because they have reason to fear,
according to the promises of the Lord,
that they are consigned
to a state of endless wo

have been verbalized, such as the speeches or sermons given by Nephi₁ (2 Ne. 32:7), Jacob (Jacob 2:31), King Limhi (Mosiah 7:23–24), or Samuel₂ (Helaman 15:2), as well as the public dialogue Nephi₂ has with the people passing by his garden (Helaman 7:15). These verses are almost all discussing the mourning that occurs because of sin. Nephi₁, for example, mourns "because of the unbelief, and the wickedness, and the ignorance, and the stiffneckedness of men" (2 Ne. 32:7).

Alma 28 refashions these two general reasons to mourn (death and unrighteousness) into three reasons to mourn. The general grief for unrighteousness remains the same, but Alma 28 divides grief for death into two categories: grief when the loved one's final state is "endless wo" (verse 11) and grief when the loved one is certainly in "a state of never-ending happiness" (verse 12). The author describes these two types of death-mourning using parallel structure, which highlights what is similar and what is different (see FIGURE 7).

Both groups have many thousands who are mourning "for the loss of their kindred." Both groups understand that their loved ones will receive according to the promises of the Lord, and that this receiving will be

65

Mourning and Never-Ending Happiness

Alma 28:12

many thousands of others truly mourn
for the loss of their kindred,
Yet they rejoice and exult in the hope, and even know,
according to the promises of the Lord,
that they are raised to dwell at the right hand of God,
In a state of never-ending happiness

FIGURE 7 Those who (truly) mourn

eternal, be it a state of endless wo (verse 11) or a state of never-ending happiness (verse 12).

The straightforward phrasing that "many thousands are mourning" in Alma 28:11 could have easily been reused to further the parallel diction, but the author chooses to break the parallelism. This deliberate break emphasizes the fact that those who rejoice that a loved one has moved on to a state of never-ending happiness do not simply mourn but "truly mourn" (verse 12). This may be a surprise. Most assume that those who mourn the loss of a loved one who made poor choices will mourn most, longest, or deepest. Presumably, there is an extra weight and pain for those who feel loss due to death and simultaneous loss due to grief of unrighteousness. Nevertheless, this chapter emphasizes that those mourning the loss of their righteous loved ones do truly mourn.

The idea that the righteous truly mourn is context-specific in meaningful ways. The original chapter xv (Alma 27–29) begins when the Anti-Nephi-Lehies "again refused to take their arms" and defend themselves (Alma 27:3), despite having already lost 1,005 of their people the first time they were attacked by the Lamanite-Amalekite-Amulonite armies (Alma 24:22). The sons of Mosiah and Alma arrange to move the people of Ammon to Jershon, where they can be protected by Nephites, but they have suffered much already, and this battle causes all to suffer more. Some might assume that the people of Ammon do not mourn the death of loved ones because they would rather "suffer death in the most aggravating and distressing manner which could be inflicted" than to defend themselves (Alma 27:29) and because they "never did look upon death with any degree of terror" (Alma 27:28). If there ever were a people whose faith in the afterlife should overcome mourning and sorrow, it is these people. And yet there can be no misunderstanding: the Anti-Nephi-Lehies are settled in Jershon (Alma 28:1), and all the people throughout all the land are mourning (Alma 28:4). Alma 28:5 reiterates that "the cry of mourning was heard among all of them."

The specific inclusion of the Anti-Nephi-Lehies broadens the idea of who mourns and deepens understanding of why people mourn. Even those who are stripped of the fear of death; who allow themselves to be "slain according to the desires of their enemies" rather than risk sin (Alma 27:3); who allow themselves, family, and friends to be massacred on multiple occasions (Alma 27:4)—even those people are part of the "great mourning and lamentation heard throughout *all* the land, among *all* the people of Nephi" (Alma 28:4; my emphasis). The Anti-Nephi-Lehies are a "highly favored people of the Lord" (Alma 27:30). They know that their loved ones "have gone to dwell with their God" (Alma 24:22), which categorizes them with those who do not just "mourn" but "truly mourn."

The mourning that occurs in Alma 28 sweeps the totality of the community and says in brief summary what becomes evident about mourning on a large scale: everyone mourns. In the Book of Mormon, individuals mourn for the deaths of individuals (Mosiah 21:9), for the deaths of groups (Ether 15:2), for the wickedness of individuals (Alma 62:2), and for the wickedness of groups

(Hel. 7:11). Groups also mourn for individuals (Mosiah 21:30), for other groups (Mosiah 28:18), for death (1 Ne. 6:35), and for wickedness (Jacob 2:31), and sometimes it is difficult to know whether mourning is for death or wickedness or both (Mosiah 7:24). Mourning crosses the cultural divide of Nephite and Lamanite (Alma 30:2) and the gender divide of male (Ether 15:3) and female (1 Ne. 5:1). It spans the gap between rich (Alma 18:43) and poor (Alma 30:2) and between old (Jacob 7:26) and young (Morm. 8:40). Mourning is a universal experience and is not limited by age, gender, culture, status, or even righteousness—the one personal circumstance to which Alma 28 might be blind.

Alma 28 discusses mourning from the point of view of the righteous, but the less-righteous also mourn. During the three days of darkness preceding the coming of Christ, there is "great mourning and howling and weeping among *all* the people *continually*" (3 Ne. 8:23; my emphasis). Those in Zarahemla are "heard to cry, saying: O that we had repented before this great and terrible day" (3 Ne. 8:24), and those in Moronihah believe that if they "had not killed and stoned the prophets, and cast them out; then would our mothers and our fair daughters, and our children" be alive (3 Ne. 8:25). If these statements are strictly true, then these people are extremely unrighteous. However, the narrator directly contradicts their lament, telling readers that "it was the more righteous part of the people who were saved, and it was they who received the prophets and stoned them not" (3 Ne. 10:12). Possibly, these people from Moronihah are lamenting collectively as a group and in fulfillment of Samuel's prophecy in Helaman 13:24–25. Their lament is not necessarily an individual confession of murder, but an admittance of communal guilt, making them "more righteous" than some, but not righteous.

Notably, it is the moment when these people connect their mourning and grief to the loss of their mothers, fair daughters, and children, that a voice is heard (3 Ne. 9:1). Only two laments are quoted at the end of 3 Nephi 8: the lament of the city of Zarahemla (verse 24) and Moronihah (verse 25). The voice addresses those who are crying in each city: Zarahemla (3 Nephi 9:3) and Moronihah (3 Nephi 9:4). Above the "howlings of the people" (3 Ne. 8:25), somehow louder than the great and terrible weeping, this voice—like the cry of lament in Alma 28—is "heard among all the inhabitants of the earth" (3 Ne. 9:1; my emphasis). All hear, but the words lightly echo the words spoken by those in Moronihah. The voice tells them that the "devil laugheth, and his angels rejoice, because of the slain of the fair sons and daughters" (3 Ne. 9:2). The voice's message also ends with connotations of family by promising to receive all who "repenteth, and cometh unto me as a little child" (3 Ne. 9:22). The message in the next chapter further connotes familial relationships, explaining that those who do not repent will find that "the places of your dwellings shall become desolate" (3 Ne. 10:7). Lamenting and mourning "continually" for three days, these less-righteous people are alone in darkness until they mourn for their loved ones (3 Ne. 8:23). When they mourn the loss of loved ones, the voice answers.

Alma 28:14 concludes with a declaration: "And thus we see the great reason of sorrow, and also of rejoicing—sorrow because of death and destruction among men, and joy because of the light of Christ unto life." The phrasing makes it easy to believe sadness and loss belong to a binary system in which there is a "great reason of sorrow" (created by "death and destruction") and an opposite "great reason...of rejoicing" (created by "joy because of the light of Christ unto life"). That reading allows two choices, and seemingly someone can choose joy and rejoicing. The verse may also distinguish a three-way differentiation: there are those who sorrow for death, and those who sorrow for destruction, and also those who rejoice. That is slightly more complex, but the choice to rejoice is still a viable, singled-out option.

But the "great reason of sorrow and also of rejoicing" is complicated by two additional "and thus we see" statements. The list and parallelism suggest that they flow continuously, each from the previous one:

"And thus we see how great the inequality
of man is because of sin and transgression"
(Alma 28:13),

"and thus we see the great call of diligence
of men to labor in the vineyards of the Lord"
(Alma 28:14),

"and thus we see the great reason of sorrow
and also of rejoicing" (Alma 28:14).

The devastation and war and loss described in this chapter is supposed to allow the reader to see inequality, but, besides the economic vulnerability of women and children, the connection between inequality and mourning is not obvious.

Interestingly, discussion about inequality following tragedy at the conclusion of the sons of Mosiah's mission is mirrored by discussion about inequality following tragedy at the conclusion of Alma's missionary journey. After the same "Lamanite" army destroys every person in Ammonihah, the church is reestablished "throughout the land" (Alma 16:15). The narrator comments that "there was no inequality among them; the Lord did pour out his Spirit on all the face of the land…that they might receive the word with joy, and as a branch be grafted into the true vine" (Alma 16:16–17). Inequality clearly includes oppressing the poor, but seemingly encompasses all sin,[10] while equality is the opposite: the state of receiving the word with joy and the Spirit pouring out. The proper response to the great inequality of man is "the great call…to labor in the vineyards of the Lord" (Alma 28:14), which is a call to resolve the inequality of sin. And it is likely that while laboring in the vineyards, those who answer the great call will come to understand the "great reason of sorrow, and also of rejoicing" (Alma 28:14).

This great reason is why the sons of Mosiah find that their missionary journeyings are a mixture of "their sufferings in the land, their sorrows, and their afflictions, and their incomprehensible joy" (Alma 28:8). Like mourning, the great reason is not about clean-cut divisions and precise lines delineating sorrow and rejoicing. Instead it flows in and through sorrow and rejoicing. The great reason creates mourners who fear (Alma 28:11) and mourners who rejoice (Alma 28:12), and most likely mourners who fear rejoicing because they know that those who truly mourn in Alma 28 are righteous rejoice-ers. Those who labor in the vineyards of the Lord will mourn, as will the widows, the fathers, the daughters, and the brothers.

Jesus promises, "Blessed are all they that mourn, for they shall be comforted" (3 Ne. 12:4). Jesus calls mourners *blessed* and says that *all* shall be comforted, including the Nephites and the Lamanites, men and women, old and young, rich and poor, unrighteous and highly favored. The Anti-Nephi-Lehies are highly favored people who have "prostrated themselves…to the earth" and allowed themselves to be slain while calling on his name for deliverance (Alma 24:21). Jesus knows "he will take upon him death," including the deaths of these 1,005 highly favored people, the deaths of other Anti-Nephi-Lehies when the "great work of destruction" takes their lives (Alma 27:4), and the deaths of all those who died in the worst war since Lehi left Jerusalem.

These deaths cause many to mourn and those who love them to truly mourn. Alma teaches that Jesus will "take upon him [the] infirmities," the mourning, the sadness, the suffering, and the pain of those left behind (Alma 7:12). Jesus suffers this "according to the flesh" (verse 13), so that he can succor every person who mourns in this life—including for grief-stricken daughters of Ishmael, mothers like Sariah who "truly...mourn" (1 Ne. 5:1) when they think their boys are lost, and Nephi, who lamented when his father died, grieving for his sins, his painful relationships with his brothers, and perhaps for the lack of empathy he displayed for his female relatives. After all, Nephi left us a story in which *he* never confuses mourning and murmuring again. Perhaps he thought we would read his story, feel compassion for his mother and his wife and her sisters, and understand that we should empathize where he did not. Are we willing to mourn with Ishmael's daughters, with Sariah, and also with Nephi?

Those who wish to avoid sorrow and mourning may wish for the simplicity of a binary world in which the great reason for rejoicing is separated from the great reason for sorrow. One could choose solely to rejoice. Unfortunately, that world is fragile. When death or destruction occurs, rejoicing flees and is replaced by sorrow. But perhaps we have misunderstood. In the Book of Mormon, mourning is consistently linked to family relationships, which should be the source of joy. And yet the loss of these relationships brings devastation. When Alma 28 invites us to "see the great reason of sorrow, and also of rejoicing" (verse 14), could it be inviting us to understand that there is only one reason?

Those who love risk sorrow and rejoicing; both are products of truly caring. To mourn is to love. To truly mourn requires truly loving. Some are willing to mourn with those who mourn, which is a call to an even deeper, more Christlike love. It is the opportunity to be a compassionate companion, one who is willing to suffer another's pain as if it were his or her own.

Ultimately, only Christ can promise to comfort *all* who mourn because only he knows their loss "according to the flesh" (Alma 7:12). The Savior's example teaches that comforting those who mourn requires understanding pain before offering comfort and certainly before offering judgment. He alone can offer to comfort all because he loves all individuals enough to mourn with each one. Those who mourn, those who truly mourn, and those who mourn with others need not be ashamed. They do not lack faith. On the contrary, the great reason for sorrow and rejoicing is not doubt but love, at times even Christlike love. It arises from faith beyond measure.

5

Even As I Have Spoken

Alma 28 establishes a setting of community mourning and ritual, which is why Alma 29 is (or should be)
a surprise. Readers suddenly encounter the personal
statement of someone wishing to be an angel, but
the chapter lacks a clear purpose, audience, or even a
speaker, though most readers presume it is spoken by
Alma. To complicate matters, after the "Amen" officially
concludes Alma 29, Alma 30:1–3 briefly reestablishes
the community's mournful setting. Alma 29 is literally
encompassed within war's destruction, surrounded by
days of mourning and fasting, and the burial of thousands. One might suppose Alma 29 should be a sermon
or prayer for this suffering community. But if Alma 29
is a community lament, we must consider why Alma,
high priest and most likely candidate to voice that
prayer, is glorying and rejoicing during a tragedy. We
could simply consider content and conclude that Alma
29 is a missionary anthem, but a rallying cry would be
untimely and insensitive. The setting frames Alma 29
inside an historical moment and predicts a structured
communal psalm of lament, yet the content of Alma 29
seems unsuitable for that mournful moment or a communal psalm of lament. Despite Alma 28 and Alma 30
firmly establishing the *when* and *where* of setting, Alma
29 is a puzzle that asks readers to reconsider their most
basic assumptions: What are these words? Who wrote

Alma 28	Commonality	Alma 30
The people of Ammon were established in the land of Jershon (1)	People of Ammon established in Jarom	The people of Ammon were established in the land of Jershon (1)
Nevertheless, the Lamanites were driven and scattered, and the people of Nephi returned again to their land (3)	Lamanites driven out of the land	And also after the Lamanites were driven out of the land (1)
And thus there was a tremendous battle; yea, even such an one as never had been known . . . yea, and tens of thousands of Lamanites were slain and scattered abroad (2)	Deaths of Lamanites	Now their dead [Lamanite] were not numbered because of the greatness of their numbers; neither were the dead of the Nephites numbered (2)
Surely this was a sorrowful day; yea, a time of solemnity, and a time of much fasting and prayer (6)	Day of fasting and prayer	And also after the days of fasting, and mourning, and prayer (2)
And the bodies of many thousands are laid low in the earth (11)	Burial	But it came to pass after they had buried their dead (2)

FIGURE 8 Inclusio framing Alma 29

them? And why? Exploring the specific setting of community mourning hints that answers are found looking backward toward the past, the tragic, and the personal.

context and form

When Alma 28 and Alma 30:1–3 mirror each other and form an inclusio—a literary "frame" of repeated words—they end up framing Alma 29 inside a specific historical setting of seemingly ritualistic community mourning. From the context before and after Alma 29, readers learn (twice) of the settlement of the people of Ammon in Jershon, the driving out of the Lamanites, the loss of life in the war, and the burial of the dead (see FIGURE 8). The narrator comments that "surely this was a sorrowful day; yea, a time of solemnity, and a time of much fasting and prayer" (Alma 28:6). Completing the inclusio, Alma 30:2 confirms that these people buried the dead, and afterward held "*the* days of fasting, and mourning, and prayer" (Alma 30:2; my emphasis). The wording seems to indicate that these are not just any days of sadness but specific days of mourning, an idea that is reinforced by noting the sorrow and solemnity that occurs.

Further evidence in the Book of Mormon sustains the idea that Nephites might have established mourning rituals and practices. When chief judge Seezoram is murdered, Helaman 9:10 describes how the "people did assemble themselves together to mourn and to fast, at the burial of the great chief judge who had been slain." This reference in Helaman does not mention prayer, which makes it unique. No one else in the Book of Mormon holds a fast without an accompanying prayer. Groups of people are much more likely than individuals to fast and pray, as in 3 Nephi 27:1 when the disciples "[gather] together and [are] united in mighty prayer and fasting" or in Alma 6:6 when the "children of

God" gather "oft, and join in fasting and mighty prayer" for the souls of unbelievers.

If Alma 28 and Alma 30 are the context of days of mourning, then what is Alma 29? Wording hints that Alma 29 was spoken, most obviously the "even as I have spoken. Amen" conclusion (verse 17), and some language indicates that an audience might be present. For example, to state "therefore we see" when no one else is present would be odd (verse 8), and wording such as "may God grant unto these, my brethren, that they may sit down in the kingdom of God" (verse 17) does not make sense without a physical gesture toward those brethren that a live audience could see. And yet, the narrator of the Book of Mormon typically explains if there is an audience present, and that is not done with Alma 29. Much of the content speaks about God instead of to God, though that alone does not disqualify it as a prayer. Nephi's psalm in 2 Nephi 4:16–35, for example, does not address God until verse 30, and other psalms of lament are similar. What are readers to do with this chapter-length embedded document?

What cannot be done is ignore or overlook it. Parallelism is the hallmark feature of ancient Hebrew poetry, including psalms.[1] In a recent study,[2] Alma 29 was the only document in the Book of Mormon with 100 percent parallelized verses, far more than Alma's brilliant retelling of his conversion in Alma 36 (76.6 percent parallelized verses) or his effective sermon in Zarahemla in Alma 5 (56.7 percent parallelized verses). Even Nephi's moving psalm of lament has only 57.14 percent parallelized verses. What this means is that the content of Alma 29 is highly crafted. Extensive time and effort are necessary to create verses that are perfectly parallel, yet subtle enough that most readers do not notice. The chance of creating such a document by happenstance is essentially nonexistent. The painstaking composition, careful positioning within a distinct historical moment, evidence of verbal communication to an audience, and wording suggestive of ritualized mourning, including community fasting and prayer, suggest that Alma 29 is that prayer. A lament would be most appropriate for the situation, although "the received form of the Hebrew Psalter was not canonized until after Lehi's lifetime." Nevertheless, "it is likely that Lehi used similar songs [psalms] as vehicles for praise and prayer in his [temple] and devotional worship."[3] In any case, Alma, high priest and record keeper, would have had access to the format of Nephi's psalm, and that is the form Alma 29 seems to follow (see chapter 6). Whatever else it is, Alma 29 is something the author created with deliberate intent and care.

author and content

Though many assume that Alma is the author of Alma 29—and that makes sense considering his role as high priest and former chief judge—most of the content in the chapter is ambiguous enough to raise doubts. Even content that seems to apply to Alma directly can often apply more generally, such as the speaker's statement that he "remember[s] the captivity of [his] fathers" (verse 11), and that he remembers that the "God of Abraham, the God of Isaac, and the God of Jacob" delivered the fathers "out of the hands of the Egyptians" (verses 11–12). The first could refer to Alma, though technically it could apply to any who were in captivity, and the second applies widely to all of Lehi's children and their descendants. Moreover, the chapter uses phraseology that Alma does not use elsewhere in the Book of Mormon, refers to experiences that he has not had, and seems too joyous to be given during a time of national crisis—a rhetorical oversight that would be abnormal for Alma.

There are significant difficulties, for example, with the use of *glory*. The speaker in Alma 29 testifies, "I know that which the Lord hath commanded me, and I glory in it" before clarifying, "I do not glory of myself, but I glory in that which the Lord hath commanded" (verse 9). Referring to glory is not abnormal for Alma; he uses the word regularly. However, Alma never uses *glory* as a verb, he never considers glory to be a normative action, and he never uses it in reference to himself. When Alma is the known speaker, he always uses *glory* as a noun and always in reference to the divine, such as, "the Son of God cometh in his glory" (Alma 5:50), or the Son's "glory shall be the glory of the Only Begotten" (Alma 9:26).[4] Alma's most direct encounter with the word *glory* is when he says that God will "raise [him] up at the last day, to dwell with him in glory" (Alma 36:28). To Alma, glory is a grace, not an action, and that grace is used only in reference to the divine.

If the author is Alma, his use of *joy* is not as troubling as *glory*, but it is peculiar. The author does "not joy" in his success but feels that his "joy is more full because of the success of my brethren" (Alma 29:14). The sentiment describes Alma, but Alma never uses *joy* as a verb elsewhere in his sermons. The author explains how bringing people to repentance or seeing them come to God makes him joyous. However, he uses the possessive pronoun *my* in four out of seven uses to tell readers about the joy *he* feels, whereas Alma's rare use of "my joy" describes how he feels *about someone else* every time but once.[5] Alma is much more likely to speak of "the joy of his Son" (Alma 33:23) or the "joyful news" of Christ's coming (Alma 13:25), usage that correlates with his overall understanding that joy is God's to give (Alma 7:4).

The author of Alma 29 speaks of overwhelming joy, effusing that his "soul is carried away, even to the separation of it from the body, as it were, so great is my joy" (Alma 29:16). Alma does feel joy, even great or exceeding joy (Alma 36:20, 21), but he regularly weakens or undermines that joy within one sentence. For example, he tells the people of Gideon that he expects to "have joy over" them, preferably without the "much afflictions and sorrow" he had in Zarahemla (Alma 7:5). He has "great joy" in his son, Shiblon, not only because of Shiblon's faithfulness and diligence but also because of his long-suffering when he was "in bonds...[and] stoned for the word's sake" (Alma 38:2–4). And Alma tells Helaman of the "exquisite and sweet" joy he felt at conversion but quickly balances that joy against "exquisite and...bitter" pain (Alma 36:21). To Helaman, Alma is speaking poetically, which may explain the balanced parallel lines, but there is no mention of joy at all in Alma's first prose conversion account. The first account describes only agony, a great need to repent, and then the relief of being "pained no more" (Mosiah 27:29).

The glory-filled exclamations and hyperbolic references to joy in Alma 29 seem more like Ammon's discourse than Alma's. Like the author of Alma 29, who uses *glory* as a verb and speaks of who ought to glory and when, Ammon exclaims, "Let us glory, yea, we will glory in the Lord;...Behold, who can glory too much in the Lord?" (Alma 26:16). Ammon's tendency to hyperbolize extends to joy, and he uses both seemingly to provoke his brother. When Aaron rebukes Ammon for boasting in his joy, Ammon, who had not used that specific word, responds by using it seven times. Ammon declares, "This is my joy" (Alma 26:37, see also Alma 29:9), speaks twice of "joy" that is "full" (Alma 26:16, 30), and is later described as being so "full" of joy that he ends up falling "*again* to the earth," having already done so previously (Alma 27:17; my emphasis). Ammon never has joy in or over someone else. He states his joy as "my" joy or "our" joy every time except once. But proposing Ammon as the author of Alma 29 only poses the same problem in reverse: suddenly there is a need to explain how Ammon could be the person discussing "sorrow upon all the face of the earth" (Alma 29:2) and struggling to be "content with the things which the Lord hath allotted unto [him]" (verse 3).

author(s) and content

Could the author of Alma 29 be both Ammon and Alma? Biblical scholarship suggests that some psalms, especially temple psalms, were "many voiced" or "antiphonal," though this typically refers to a priest interacting with a chorus, or perhaps a chorus interacting with another chorus.[6] Psalms, especially psalms of lament, may also be "multivoiced" prayers (prayer with more than one speaker) or "dialogic" prayers (a prayer that switches purpose and primary audience).[7] Some of these psalms are "dialogic" because they alternate between "effective" prayer (a prayer in which making oneself heard by God is the primary purpose though an audience may happen to overhear) and "efficacious" prayer (a more didactic prayer in which having an audience hear something is the primary purpose though the prayer is ostensibly addressed to God).[8] Perhaps Alma 29 was written or spoken by different people—possibly Alma as primary author while Ammon wrote or spoke part of the chapter. There is a change from the more confessional beginning to the more audience-oriented conclusion. Perhaps Alma used more Ammon-like words to differentiate when he was directing his prayer toward the audience (efficacious).

Another possibility is that Alma's rhetoric changed either purposefully or inadvertently. Alma is rhetorically gifted enough to adjust his speech patterns, but why would a capable rhetor give this speech after a catastrophic battle and stunning loss of life? Alma's style might have changed slowly and inadvertently over time as he experienced missions, served as chief judge, and watched his people die in ongoing battles and bloodshed, but that does not explain the phrasing or references to experiences he has not had. Readers are left in a quandary. With a mix of phrases and ideas that may or may not be Alma's and concerns about tone and style, and yet with historical context weighing heavily in Alma's favor, most assume that Alma 29 was written by Alma. If readers tentatively adopt Alma as author, they answer the question of who said these words, but why someone said these words is more complicated.

Alma and silence

Distracted by the missionary adventures of Ammon and his brethren among the Lamanites, readers might not realize that five years have passed since they last heard Alma preach. The last speech he gave was in Ammonihah, after which he provides revelatory military strategy and heals Zeezrom (Alma 15:10), and then there is silence until Alma 29. The lack of direct speech is not from illness or disability. In the intervening time, the text indicates that Alma ministered to Amulek (Alma 15:18), continued his missionary work (Alma 16:13), and discovered the returning sons of Mosiah (Alma 17:1; 27:16). Yet Alma does not resurface as a known speaker until Alma 30:32 when he argues with Korihor, and he does not resurface as a public speaker until he cries out to God in distress about the Zoramites in Alma 31:25–35.

Direct speech is not the only silence. Authorship and the marking of time also become nebulous. Authorship is established in the text prior to the speeches at Ammonihah, such as in Alma 9:1, which quotes Alma:

"And again, I, Alma...began to preach unto them." Mormon is presumably the author-editor, summarizing from Alma 10:31 until Alma's disappearance, given that these chapters refer to Alma in the third person rather than as a first-person actor. Superscriptions, the short summary paragraphs above random chapter headings in the Book of Mormon, are found during Alma's record keeping responsibilities above Alma 1, 5, 7, 9, 17, and 21, before disappearing until Alma 36, 38, and 39. The superscriptions above 1, 7, 9, and 17 name Alma as record keeper, and the superscription over Alma 45 indicates that what follows is from Helaman's record. Yet, except for Alma 35:16 stating that Alma's words to his sons are "according to his own record," in-text indicators of Alma's authorship after Ammonihah are missing, and, moreover, intervening superscriptions do not indicate the record's authorship.

Moreover, precise dating is absent from Alma 16–28, though Mormon is typically meticulous as he chronicles dates. Mormon even punctuates his record with verses such as Helaman 11:35–38 that simply name year after year, something that would be impossible had they not been recorded. This is why the lack of precise dates is notable. Dates were specific and clear early in Alma's ministry. In fact, the Book of Mormon records only nine dates with day, month, and year. Intriguingly, Ammonihah-related dates are consistently precise. Readers know the date of Alma's second arrival in Ammonihah (Alma 10:6); the date when the chief judge, teachers, and lawyers come for the last time to mock and abuse (Alma 14:23); and the date when Lamanites destroy Ammonihah, which is noted twice in Alma 16:1. After such precision, Alma's story wraps up in a terse half of a chapter that vaguely summarizes three years and then transitions into the story of the sons of Mosiah and their Lamanite mission. The Lamanite mission occurs concurrently with Alma 1–16. Perhaps the sons of Mosiah did not keep records with dates because their mission is also relatively unmarked by time or consistent narrator identification. These details point to the past, particularly toward Ammonihah, the last concrete moment when Alma recorded dates, spoke publicly, and clearly authored the record.

alma 29 and Ammonihah

Alma 29 does not refer explicitly to the moment when dates and authorship were last distinct, but allusions connect this chapter with Alma's experience in Ammonihah. Verse one begins, "O that I were an angel, and could have the wish of mine heart." Alma is the only person in scripture who discusses the "wishes" of his "heart," and the only other place he does so is while finishing his sermon in Ammonihah, saying, "I wish from the inmost part of my heart" (Alma 13:27). The wish of Alma's heart is to speak with a "voice of thunder" like an angel and preach the "plan of redemption" (Alma 29:2), which is what he tried to do in Ammonihah. Five times in Ammonihah, Alma spoke of the "plan of redemption" (Alma 12:25, 26, 30, 32, 33), though he had never used that phrase before, and he "cried with a mighty voice" for the people to repent (Alma 13:21), specifically mentioning that angels declare this message (Alma 13:22, 24, 25, 26). At Ammonihah, Alma explains that the gospel is declared to "all nations" by the "mouth of angels," even to "them that are scattered abroad upon the face of the earth" (Alma 13:22). In Alma 29, Alma asks himself why he desires to be an angel and "speak unto all the ends of the earth" (verse 7). What Alma's heart wishes to do is cry repentance, and in Alma 13:27 he begs the Ammonihahites with "great anxiety even unto pain" that they will "not procrastinate the day of [their] repentance."

But the people in Ammonihah not only do not repent, they also burn women and children in their fires. Amulek implores Alma to "exercise the power of God" and halt the "awful scene" of human sacrifice (Alma 14:10). Other scenes in the Book of Mormon are horrible or full of carnage and bloodshed, but only Ammonihah, the battle in Alma 28 (verse 10), and the closing battle of the Book of Mormon are awful (Moro. 5:8). There are many indications that Alma is thinking about Ammonihah while writing and speaking Alma 29. Why he would be thinking of Ammonihah in Alma 29 coincides with an explanation of why Alma 29 sounds so little like Alma.

Alma and Ammonihah

The focus of the rising action and climax in Ammonihah is Alma's and Amulek's faith in Christ, which miraculously saves them. With the power of God, Alma and Amulek break the "strong cords" with which they are bound (Alma 14:4), and then they come "forth out of the prison...not hurt" (verse 28), though the earth shakes, the prison walls fall down, and everyone else is killed. It is miraculous, but the text most likely means that they were not hurt further in the prison collapse. Alma was reviled, spit upon, and cast out the first time he preached (Alma 8:13). When he returns, Amulek joins him, and both are bound with cords for "many days" and imprisoned (Alma 14:23). At very least, the strong cords that bind Alma and Amulek damage their skin, similarly to the strong cords binding Aaron and Muloki; Ammon was exceedingly sorrowful to find them "naked, and their skins...worn exceedingly because of being bound with strong cords" (Alma 20:29). Alma and Amulek were also deprived of food and water, stripped of clothing, and physically abused by repeated slaps and punches. They were not killed in the prison collapse, but they do not leave Ammonihah unharmed.

More than physical harm, however, the story focuses on the mocking, distressing words spoken by the chief judge and the "many lawyers, and judges, and priests, and teachers" (Alma 14:18). The focus of these details hints that the psychological wounds are more haunting than the physical ones. The narrator specifies the setting: Alma and Amulek are bound with cords, carried to the edge of the martyrdom, and there forced to watch while women and children are still "consuming" in the fire (verse 10). They remain beside the smoldering fire until the chief judge of the land returns and slaps them "with his hand upon their cheeks," possibly a gesture of contempt or a means of centering attention on himself (verse 14). The chief judge asks, "After what ye have seen, will ye preach again unto this people, that they shall be cast into a lake of fire and brimstone?" (verse 14).

This is not a random question. It is targeted directly at Alma and aimed to damage him as much as possible. The chief judge probably does not care what metaphor Alma used to preach repentance, except that this metaphor was useful in escalating Alma's pain. The judge's question seems targeted to remind Alma of his prophecy that the torment of the unrepentant "shall be as a lake of fire and brimstone, whose flame ascendeth up forever and ever" (Alma 12:17). The judge and the people of Ammonihah guarantee that Alma sees friends die. They guarantee that Amulek, the man an angel promised would be blessed by Alma's presence, is beside Alma. Bound with strong cords and brought to the fire while the flames are blazing, Alma and Amulek are forced to witness women and children—most likely including Amulek's family—be burned to death, an agonizing way to die. Still not content, the chief judge ensures that Alma understands the brutal irony at the heart of this horror: Alma's unfortunate gospel metaphor about a lake of fire and brimstone prompts the literal lake of fire and brimstone that burns before his eyes.

The violence revolves around words, ideas, and metaphor in ways that are vicious, deliberate, and personal. As a former unbeliever, Alma knows that his preconversion beliefs inform the philosophies of Ammonihah's citizens. Though the narrator blames Nehor, the people of Ammonihah have more in common with the unbelievers than with Nehor (see chapter 3). Alma came to reclaim these people, but they know who Alma was, and they know how to hurt him. He preaches of fiery punishment (Alma 12:17), watches his words become horrifyingly real (Alma 14:8–11), and then is told that he is to blame for the deaths he witnesses—or, at least, that his words sparked the idea (Alma 14:14). Ammonihah's citizens aim to torture Alma in horrifyingly inhumane ways, and the final twist is telling him that his rhetoric, his hallmark skill, is the cause. They purposefully mock him by killing "whosoever had been taught to believe" in their inferno, as if killing women and children is a grotesque literary joke, a witty massacre. Events much less dramatic, much less pointed, and much less personal than Ammonihah can haunt someone, even traumatize.

When the chief judge asks his question about a lake of fire and brimstone, Alma and Amulek "answered him nothing" (Alma 14:17). In the prison, the men are questioned "about many words; but they answered them nothing" (verse 18). When the chief judge commands them to speak, "they answered nothing" (verse 19). Silence can be a rational choice, but it can also be a response to shocking trauma. *Trauma*, the Greek word for *wound*, occurs when events overwhelm the mind.[9] What a person's eyes saw or ears heard or body felt is recorded in the brain, but the mind is unable to process or integrate the event into a person's understanding of reality. The memories are in someone's brain, but they are scattered and recorded in fragments. The event becomes unspeakable, each memory disconnected from other memories of the event, and

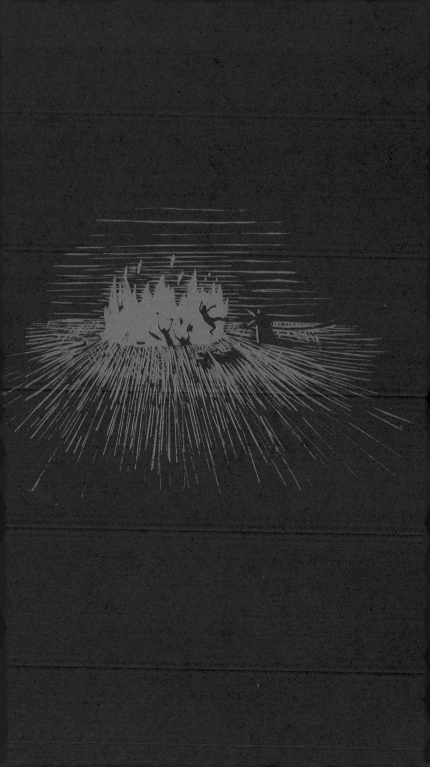

likely remembered as feeling or emotion or image rather than in words and language.

Hearing that his words ignited the atrocity silences Alma for days. He eventually speaks in the prison and later to Zeezrom and to the widowers in Sidom, but there is at least one phrase he will never say again in the Book of Mormon: *lake of fire and brimstone*. These events redefine his vocabulary. Moreover, they redefine the vocabulary of the entire Book of Mormon. The extent of the shock and distress caused by Ammonihah's fires is encapsulated in the fact that this well-used metaphor of hell disappears from the Nephite records. Many spoke of this hell previously: Nephi (2 Ne. 28:23), King Benjamin (Mosiah 3:27), and Jacob on multiple occasions (2 Ne. 9:16, 26; Jacob 3:11; 6:12), but after people burn women and children alive in a lake of fire and brimstone, the words *lake of fire and brimstone* are never spoken again by anyone in the Book of Mormon.

If Alma 29 is Alma's first attempt to articulate the horror he witnessed at Ammonihah, then readers must be exquisitely sensitive. Those who are attempting to process trauma need patient acceptance. Alma comes because his people need him to speak, but he does not bring his well-known articulateness or his preconversion flattering words or perhaps even his own words. He brings five years of textual silence. Contemporary readers cannot know with certainty whether Alma's silence is caused by traumatic unspeakableness or by rhetorical choice, but either way he has lost words. While Alma 29 can be interpreted as Alma's celebration of his love of missionary work, doubtless one of many inspired interpretations, Alma's record hints that this is a psalm of lament and that Alma is the voice of the people as they lament their losses after a devastating war. He may be trying to voice a typical lament: expressing grief and collective loss, praying that God will comfort these people and give them hope, and finishing with praise. But his words strain their meanings, hinting that the trauma of Ammonihah remains raw and painful, hinting that this public moment merged with his personal woundedness.

Why Alma responds is because sons and daughters and fathers and mothers are mourning, and a high priest should support his people. That is why the most likely author of the psalm in Alma 29 is Alma, himself. He does not lament the pain of his battle-scarred people; he laments by returning to where he last spoke and what he last said. *What* he speaks about is glory and joy and repentance, inappropriate messages that will be misunderstood if readers do not listen carefully. If Alma sounds too optimistic for the setting, it is because where he last spoke was Ammonihah, what he last said called people to repentance, and what happened because of his words was devastating. Crying repentance is what angels do that there "might not be more sorrow upon all the face of the earth" (Alma 29:2), but crying repentance might also spark Ammonihah-sized fires that burn everything they touch, multiplying sorrow, death, and destruction.

Ultimately, *how* may be the question that matters most. How is one to speak again after trauma? How are words possible after a chief judge asks, "Will ye preach again unto this people, that they shall be cast into a lake of fire and brimstone?" (Alma 14:14).

Silence is Alma's answer. The hatred and vindictiveness bring Alma to a quiet place where time moves without marking, where the narrator cannot explain who is speaking, and where Alma seems to be struggling to speak at all. If Alma did not know before, he does now: following the command of an angel does not indicate that all will be well; repenting does not mean that guilt or shame for past sin will not reemerge years later and slap harder than a malicious judge; obedience does not prevent a community of wicked people from lighting a fire and burning innocents. The lessons are harsh; they tutored Alma into stillness. But to help his grieving people, Alma painstakingly crafts a psalm, relying on Nephi and possibly Ammon for help. What he produces is 100 percent parallelized—and unlike anything he has uttered before.

Alma's strangely unfitting words convey a message—perhaps unintentionally—about how he is able to bring himself to this moment. Alma's "holy calling, to preach the word unto this people," requires words and voice, and it invokes both vertical and horizontal contact (Alma 29:13). He must pray vertically to God and then wait for revelation to come down. He must listen horizontally to his people and then speak the words of God to them. He interacts with God in the give-and-take of prayer and revelation, as well with his people in the push-and-pull of individual and community. This holy calling puts Alma at the crossroads, and that is where Alma's angel reappears. On the road from Ammonihah to Aaron, Alma is commanded to go back. He "return[s] speedily" and walks straight into a hell created by his people using his words (Alma 8:18). Five obscure years pass. Alma hears the cry of mourning, and he responds to his community. Alma may not perform his holy calling perfectly in Alma 29. It is a heavy cross to carry, but he picks it up. Though he will never utter some words again, Alma finds that the "wish of [his] heart" is to "*speak* with the trump of God," to go forth with a "*voice* to shake the earth," and to "*cry*," and to "*declare* . . . as with the voice of thunder" (Alma 29:1–2; my emphasis). Alma wants to speak again.

6

O That I Were an Angel

Offering a public lament in a war-torn society would be challenging for a resilient and healthy person. Alma likely begins his speech wounded and in pain. ☞ But he concludes powerfully, calling on God to grant his prayer "according to my words, even as I have spoken," the first time he uses this oath-like phrasing, though not the last (Alma 29:17). How does this happen over the course of one short sermon? Alma 29 is the locus of change, the point marking a shift from shock to verbal strength. Articulating a psalm of lament for his community that parallels Nephi's personal psalm of lament seems to move Alma toward healing. Alma's lament provides insight into the personal pain and healing of a high priest of the church of God, and it introduces readers to an ancient spiritual practice that can initiate healing communication with the divine.

Understanding what constitutes a psalm of lament is the basis of understanding how Alma 29 helps Alma. Form-critical analysis provides the vocabulary and tools to pull apart Alma's structure and his words. Analyzing the content and function of the parts demonstrates the theological and healing work that can occur in each—and yet adding the parts together within the overall structure becomes more than the simple sum of the sections. Lamenting is not a description or story about what

☞ Though textual evidence cannot prove conclusively that Alma found Ammonihah to be intensely disturbing, even traumatic, this chapter will proceed with that assumption for the purposes of explaining psalms of lament and their potential healing affect.

96

should be done. It is an example of doing it. Lament is the pathway, itself. 🖝 The words of Alma 29 are the rhetorical remains of an emotional journey, but they are not a fossil. The words of lament do not just tell a story of what moved Alma; they are what moves Alma. Naturally, much more is involved than one psalm; the loss of the *lake of fire and brimstone* phrase from the entire Book of Mormon indicates that others recognize the difficulty of healing. Writing a lament—and in Alma's situation, most likely verbalizing that lament—is not a cure-all. Yet it can play a part in healing the stunned silence left when grievous harm overwhelms a person. Readers who walk the pathway created by Alma's words and the words of other psalmists gain empathy and understanding for him, as well as insight into the path of lament, a journey that begins in a place of woundedness and ends with praise.

individual psalm of lament

When Alma speaks after five long years, he uses odd words structured like Nephi's psalm. Sidney B. Sperry labeled 2 Nephi 4:16–35 as the Book of Mormon's "single psalm" in 1947.[1] Fifty years later, another Latter-day Saint scholar used biblical authority Hermann Gunkel's five-element structure to more specifically classify Nephi's psalm as an individual psalm of lament,[2] since it follows Gunkel's proposed structure with its 1. invocation, 2. complaint or lament, 3. confession of trust, 4. petition, and 5. vow of praise. Although Alma 29 is structured similarly, even following Nephi's psalm in its extra turn back toward complaint or lament (see

🖝 Research shows that psychological, emotional, and even physical benefits can be gained by participation in personal expressive writing, something that I have seen in both my personal and my professional life. However, I (the author) am not a health-care professional. Readers should consult their health-care professionals for their specific needs.

1. Invocation **Alma 29:1**

   2. Complaint or lament **Alma 29:1–3**

      3. Confessions of trust **Alma 29:4–9**

         4. Petitions **Alma 29:10–18**

            5. Vows of trust/promise of praise **Alma 29:14–17**

FIGURE 9 Gunkel's structure of lament

FIGURE 9), it is not what Sperry would call a "true psalm in both form and idea." Few would say that Alma 29 "lays bare to us the very depths" of Alma's soul or "betrays deep religious feeling" like Nephi's psalm does. The content of Alma 29 is less personal and less lamenting than 2 Nephi 4, although that can be appropriate for many individual psalms of lament. As a biblical scholar explains, even hundreds of years ago, the "traditional parts [of a psalm of lament] enabled individual sufferers to put their own personal suffering into a lament which had been used already by their parents and grandparents. And these forms let them hide the suffering which was theirs and theirs alone in a lament which had been brought before God a thousand times before."[3] In following Nephi's structure, and yet doing so with reticence and verbal ambiguity, Alma is following the long-standing tradition of lamentation.

invocation
ALMA 29:1

1 O that I were an angel, and could have the wish of
   mine heart, ...

The psalm begins, "O that I were an angel"—a phrase that is the first and most obvious indication that this chapter is an individual lament. Use of first-person pronouns denote personal lament, whereas communal laments, such as Psalm 80, use plural personal pronouns. Still, without context, the "I" is a disorienting switch from the previous chapter. But what readers may think is a grammatical error is called *enallage*, the practice of abruptly switching pronouns in either person, gender, or number. Biblical psalms switch easily, as do the verses leading up to Alma 29:1. The original chapter break joins chapters 27–29, so there is a natural progression toward the personal. Alma 28:1–12 distances readers with the use of third-person plural pronouns: readers can sympathize, but "they"—the Nephite people—are mourning, and the reader is not. Alma 28:13–14 switches to "we," which makes it seem as if the audience agrees with the "and thus we see" statements. After sympathizing with them about their tragic losses, then being drawn in as the communal we, the audience is swept forward into Alma 29, most likely identifying with the narrator, the "I," since there is no other character to identify with. The reader draws closer with the use of increasingly personal pronouns, and the writer is also drawing closer, a threatening prospect if painful memories are waiting.

Pain could explain the brevity of the invocation, "O that I were an angel," though some scholars question whether a meager "O" is a real invocation. While many psalms, especially communal psalms, have longer, more reverential beginnings, individual psalms of lament are known for their unpretentious invocations; they may begin with a single Hebrew word. These succinct beginnings convey desperation, not disrespect; they convey familiarity, not foreignness. A year later, Alma again addresses the Lord abruptly. He cries out, "O, how long, O Lord…?" (Alma 31:26). Alma speaks to his God in informal language and with a heartfelt exclamation, seeming as if he is well acquainted with his God.[4] Like Nephi, Alma knows that his God is approached with "no hypocrisy and no deception" (2 Nephi 31:13). In great need, Alma—or anyone—can cry out abruptly. The invocation may remind Alma who God is, who he is to God, and why he assumed God would hear a pained, honest plea for help.

The process of lament allows for some variation but is generally standardized and identifiable. It may not be a coincidence that Alma returned to public discourse with a lament. Trauma memories are scattered yet often vivid. They can terrorize not only with their content but also with their unordered and possibly unknown depth and breadth. Someone facing fragmented hurt can feel safe with lament's rules, structure, and guaranteed ending. No matter what negative emotion begins a lament, the psalm ends in praise—and a writer knows this before one word of abrupt invocation is written. If someone fears being overwhelmed or lost in negative emotion, the secure ending may provide enough safety to begin.

complaint or lament
ALMA 29:1–2

1 ... that I might go forth and speak
      with the trump of God,
      with a voice to shake the earth,
      and cry repentance unto every people!

2   Yea, I would declare unto every soul,
      as with the voice of thunder,
      repentance and the plan of redemption,
      that they should repent and come unto our God,
      that there might not be more sorrow
      upon all the face of the earth

100

After the invocation, individual psalms of lament typically move into "complaint" or "lament." Those who focus on psalms of praise may be startled by the honest and expressive emotion in lament. Psalm 13:1, for example, demands, "How long wilt thou forget me, O Lord? For ever? How long wilt thou hide thy face from me?" while Psalm 88:14 aggressively questions, "Lord, why castest thou off my soul? Why hidest thou thy face from me?" These laments accuse the Lord of neglect during times of trouble and may insist that something is wrong with God's caretaking of his covenant people.[5] A psalmist might also rage against his or her "enemies," petitioning God to throw "down into the pit of destruction" these "bloody and deceitful men" (Ps. 55:23) or pleading with God to "Arise, O Lord; save me, O my God" and do so by "smit[ing] all mine enemies upon the cheek bone" or by "[breaking] the teeth of the ungodly" (Ps. 3:7).

Not all psalms of lament are angry—some may be despairing (see Ps. 88:4), and some may be sad (see Ps. 102:2). Alma 29 is not insistent, demanding, or accusatory; Alma simply laments his wish for a trumpet and the voice of an angel (Alma 29:2), which he wants so he can speak "with a voice to shake the earth, and cry repentance unto every people" (Alma 29:1). Alma may be alluding to his own angel, who spoke "with a voice of thunder, which caused the earth to shake" (Mosiah 27:11). Because he understands how powerful and repentance-inducing an earth-shaking angelic visitation can be, Alma yearns for that same power so that he can "cry repentance" (Alma 29:1) and "declare . . . the plan of redemption" to "every soul, as with the voice of thunder" (verse 2). Sorrow for sin is often the impetus compelling a prophet's lament, but Alma 29 is lamenting from a different historical vantage point. With "the bodies of many thousands . . . moldering in heaps upon the face of the earth" (Alma 28:11), Alma's desire to be an angel is an expression of grief more than missionary zeal, a lamentation about death and destruction more than wickedness. What he wants is to proclaim the gospel, but why he wants to proclaim it is because there is so much "sorrow upon all the face of the earth" (Alma 29:2).

These words are lamenting not only this devastating war but likely Alma's personal pain, as well. The scattered trauma memories may be unintegrated into a narrative sequencing, literally unspeakable in a story format. But memories that are a mixture of feelings and pictures can harmonize with poetry's imagistic style. Alma never says Ammonihah in this lament, but he writes metaphorically and creatively of *angels* and *wishes* and *voices of thunder*, of preaching to all people of *all nations* wherever they are *on the earth*, and of an *awful scene* and the *plan of redemption*. All of these phrases are used in the more difficult, more sad introductory parts of this lament, and all have unique connections to Ammonihah (see chapter 5). Though Alma does not refer to that city, its people, or its fires, he seems to be thinking of what happened there.

complaint or lament—first "turn"
ALMA 29:3–4

3   But behold,
       I am a man, and do sin in my wish;
       for I ought to be content
       with the things which the Lord hath allotted
       unto me.

4   I ought not to harrow up in my desires
       the firm decrees of a just God, ...

Alma moves forward from lamenting by "turning," or pivoting around the word *but*. *But* marks change, contrast, or modification; in lament, it denotes a shift or "transition from lamentation."[6] In this psalm, *but* turns Alma away from sorrow and his desire to be an angel and toward a judgmental absolute: "But behold, I am a man, and do sin in my wish" (Alma 29:3). Readers may not notice that this switch is a change to the step Gunkel called Confessions of Trust because it is not obvious that confessing that he is wrong and sinful is Alma's way of confessing that he *trusts* God is right. Nephi's psalm also turns away from lamenting "the temptations and the sins which do so easily beset [him]" (2 Ne. 4:18). Pivoting on the word "nevertheless," Nephi announces, "my heart groaneth because of my sins; nevertheless, I know in whom I have trusted" (2 Ne. 4:19).

Nephi's movement toward "Confessions of Trust" is unmistakable, but Alma takes a slight detour before confessing what he knows about God. The devastation of war is the immediate cause of the lament, but Alma focuses on personal responsibility rather than accusing God. Where Nephi is sorrowing because of his weaknesses and sins and calling himself a "wretched man" (2 Ne. 4:17), Alma merely wishes he were an angel. It is a small complaint. Few notice he is complaining, and that is why this inward turn is surprising. Why the self-condemnation over a complaint that barely sounds complaining? That he accuses himself of sin provides insight into Alma's thinking that he may not have meant to reveal. Telling himself that he "ought to be content with the things which the Lord hath allotted me" means the opposite: Alma is not content with what the Lord has allotted to him (Alma 29:3). Telling himself that he "ought not to harrow up in my desires the firm decree of a just God" means that he is indeed harrowing up in his desires something other than what the Lord decreed for him (verse 4).

Alma's lament is not as angry or aggressive or despairing as many biblical laments sound—but he wants to be an angel and to do more work than the work the Lord has assigned him (verse 6). He wants to serve God, but God has apparently decreed (firmly) that he cannot. His honesty leaves him in a place that is confusing, yet realistic. Why does he think he should be content? Why is he not? Why does he want to be an angel, and why does God say no?

confessions of trust
ALMA 29:4–9

4 ... for I know that he granteth ...
    their desire,
    whether it be unto death or unto life;
    yea, I know that he allotteth unto men, ...
    according to their wills,
    whether they be unto salvation or unto destruction.

5 Yea, and I know that
    good and evil have come before all men;
    he that knoweth not
    good from evil is blameless;
    but he that knoweth
    good and evil, to him it is
    given according to his desires,
    whether he desireth good or evil,
    life or death, joy or remorse of conscience.

Like Nephi, Alma asks difficult questions in his lament—questions that Alma attempts to answer as his Confessions of Trust. He testifies of what he knows to be true; Alma says he knows that people are given according to their desires, that God "allotteth unto men...according to their wills," and that the Lord "*decreeth* unto them *decrees*,... according to their wills" (Alma 29:4; my emphasis). And yet Alma desired to be an angel, and God decreed that he could not. Alma counsels himself to be content with what the Lord has allotted rather than to be upset about his unfulfilled desire to be like an angel, but he testified that God decrees and people receive what they desire. Something is not making sense, and writing it makes that obvious.

confessions of trust—second "turn"
ALMA 29:6–9

6   Now, seeing that I know these things,
      why should I desire more...?

7   Why should I desire that I were an angel...?

8   I know that which the
      Lord hath commanded me,
      and I glory in it.
      I do not glory of myself,
      but I glory in that
      which the Lord hath commanded me;
      yea, and this is my glory...

In both 2 Nephi 4 and Alma 29, there is a secondary "turn." Both psalms express this second turn using a time-oriented transitional phrase, a visual metaphor for knowledge, and a conditional statement that leads into a series of "why" questions. Nephi questions, "O *then*, if I have *seen* so great things...*why* should my heart weep?" (2 Ne. 4:26; my emphasis) while Alma 29:6 queries, "*Now, seeing* that I know these things, why should I desire more than to perform the work to which

105

I have been called?" (my emphasis). Contextually the vision-related diction flows from the previous verses; it also alludes to the introductory verses when Nephi contemplates the things he has "seen and heard" (2 Ne. 4:16) and to Alma's verses listing "and thus we see" statements (Alma 28:14) (see chapter 4). With these tidy transitions that echo their overall themes, both psalmists then ask a series of rhetorical why questions.

Psalmists' most popular questions are Why? and How long?—questions that technically ask for an explanation and about duration. If asked in prideful defiance, either could be labeled as murmuring, but neither can be judged as faithless. Questioning God about why something happens demonstrates faith that he is there and hope that he has an answer. Moreover, underlying both questions is a plea for God to make sense of suffering. Psalmists ask How long? likely as an expression of longing for pain to end but also as a question about why pain must continue. At the root of both questions is Why? To ask why is to ask for meaning, to ask God to make sense of suffering. Pain and suffering prompt the question, but it is meaninglessness that is unendurable.

In a variation from biblical psalms, the why questions Nephi and Alma ask are not petitions for the Lord to make meaning of their pain. Both turn their rhetorical questions inward, the least common of the three dimensions of questioning typical in psalms. Alma is not expecting God or anyone else to answer when he asks rhetorically, "Why should I desire that I were an angel, that I could speak unto all the ends of the earth?" (Alma 29:7). Nephi is chastising himself when he queries, "Why should I yield to sin?" and "Why am I angry because of mine enemy?" (2 Ne. 4:27). This enemy-question may be not only Nephi's most compellingly honest question but also the most uncomfortable question for a modern reader. The psalms have a jarring number of references to "enemies," far more than in any other book in scripture. Christians are taught, "Love your enemies" (Matt. 5:44). We often "take this a leap further than Jesus did and say that we have no enemies."[7] Leaping past the naming of an enemy may be a way of leaping past the pain without going through the process, a way to "forgive" that looks strikingly similar to denial. If psalmists are to love their enemies, the enemy behavior or words must be named as such first. That is what lament can do.

Though Nephi's questions are self-directed, he wrote his psalm on the plates, assuming readership. And while Alma's psalm follows Nephi's individual psalm structure, it seems to have been spoken before his community. Both state their why questions rhetorically, apparently assuming their audience will agree. After all, why should Nephi "give way to temptations?" Why should he or anyone "yield to sin"? Why should Alma presumptuously wish to be an angel?

Despite these psalmists' suppositions, it is premature to think the audience will approve. Unlike most biblical psalms, these psalms are embedded in their narrative context and setting, their so-called "situation in life." Asking why within a narrative context opens the possibility for readers to question the psalmist's questions. Are these self-condemning accusations realistic? Are they fair? Nephi's father has just died, his older brothers have turned murderous again, he is far from Jerusalem, and he has an ever-growing family depending on him for protection. Nephi asks sincerely why his heart is weeping and why his soul is lingering in the valley of sorrow, but readers may ask why his heart should not weep and why his soul should not linger in the valley of sorrow. Similarly, thousands of dead bodies are buried and thousands more are heaped upon the earth. Readers may wonder why Alma should not "desire more than to perform the work to which [he has] been called" (Alma 29:6). The circumstances are horrifying. If Alma could have helped, shouldn't he have been allowed to do so?

Acknowledging and honoring a psalmist's questions is a part of the process, and both Nephi and Alma follow the structure, asking questions from a place of honesty, God-focused spirituality, history, and other personal factors. Both direct those questions inward rather than outward at God or at others. But their psalms presume an audience of readers or listeners, and that displays the psalmists' accusatory thinking to others—and possibly to themselves. Psalmists may need to reconsider: is their self-condemnation entirely appropriate? The writing process itself and more especially the realization that others may hear or read the lament encourages metacognition, the conscious thinking about one's thoughts. This can be a healthy emotional process, as it seemed to be for Nephi and Alma for many reasons. At very least, the structure means psalmists cannot remain in their own minds in an endless loop of self-accusative questions, an impulse that writing diminishes and that having an audience seriously discourages. Moving through the process means taking the why questions seriously—and then either answering them or petitioning the Lord for help, or both. Notably, Nephi's why questions become the basis of a significant shift: they move Nephi from talking about God to Nephi talking to God.

Nephi's structure invites a psalmist to express and question suffering, turn toward praise, and then return to pain—a "double-turn." Alma can re-ask and re-answer his questions, and that process seems to change him. When Alma asks in Alma 29:7, "Why should I desire that I were an angel, that I could speak unto all the ends of the earth?" he is asking a question he has already considered (verse 1) and has already answered

108

(verse 3). This question apparently weighs heavily on him, and his first answer, "I am a man and do sin" is insufficient. After lamenting with numerous allusions to Ammonihah, Alma re-asks and re-answers, explaining the second time that "the Lord doth grant unto all nations, of their own nation and tongue, to teach his word" (verse 8). Though the Book of Mormon regularly discusses teaching "all nations," Alma does not. He only refers to this effort twice: here (Alma 29:8) and at Ammonihah (Alma 13:22).

Considering the numerous allusions, Alma may be thinking Why Ammonihah? during his first answer (that he is a man and a sinner) and also during his second (that the Lord sends people to teach). Given the understated wording and delicacy of the allusion, any conclusions are tentative, but the critical element may be Alma's realization that "the Lord" sent him "to teach his word" (Alma 29:8). His angel commanded Alma to return and "say unto them, except they repent the Lord God will destroy them" (Alma 8:16). If the interpretation and weaponizing of his words about a lake of fire and brimstone have tormented him with self-blame, then it would be a blessed relief to understand that although he may blame himself, God does not.

The parts of lament are helpful for a psalmist, but the structured process—especially Nephi's restrained alteration, the double-turn—may be especially appropriate in a religious community that values happiness and orderliness. This double opportunity to speak of one's suffering is a double affirmation that God accepts the authentic anger, the anguish, the candid doubt, and the depression of psalmists. He accepts Alma's wish to be an angel (Alma 29:1), and when Alma says it again, he accepts it again (verse 7). Alma can question the Lord's allotment and express discontent

with the things the Lord has decreed (verses 3–4), and
he can question the same thing again (verse 6). He can
do so within the safety of lament, knowing that the
same God will listen again. But Alma will also have to
answer again. Doing so seems to help him understand
that self-accusations are not necessarily God's answer.

petitions
ALMA 29:10–18

10   And behold,
  when I see many of my brethren truly penitent . . .
  then is my soul filled with joy;
  then do I remember what the Lord
  has done for me . . .
  yea, then do I remember
  his merciful arm . . .

11   Yea, and I also remember
  the captivity of my fathers; . . .
  the Lord did deliver them out of bondage, . . .
  yea, the Lord God . . .
  did deliver them out of bondage.

12   Yea, I have always remembered
  the captivity of my fathers;
  and *that same God* who delivered them
  out of the hands of the Egyptians
  did deliver them out of bondage.

13   Yea, and *that same God*
  did establish his church among them;
  yea, and *that same God*
  hath called me by a holy calling, . . .
  and hath given me much success, . . .

110

Although petitions are the expected next step in Gunkel's structure, Alma begins narrating key historical stories. Recalling various occasions of past deliverance is not straightforward petitioning but can work in a similar manner. Alma notes the captivity and deliverance of his "fathers" (Alma 29:11), as well as the captivity of the Israelites and their deliverance (verse 12). Remembering those events helps Alma "remember what the Lord has done for me, yea, even that he hath heard my prayer; yea, then do I remember his merciful arm which he extended towards me" (verse 10). The past can strengthen faltering faith in the present. In this instance, the repetition is especially effective. Alma often repeats that same God (verses 11, 12, and 13—twice) and delivering out of bondage (verse 11—twice, and 12). It is almost impossible to misunderstand: Alma believes that the same God who delivered him and others before can deliver out of bondage again. The past serves as a reminder to Alma and his audience that God can be trusted in the present, and it may even serve as a delicate reminder to God: he can deliver his people.[8]

vows of trust / promise of praise
ALMA 29:14–17

14   But I do not joy
       in my own success alone,
       but my joy is more full

16   Now, when I think
       of the success of these my brethren . . .
       so great is my joy.
17   And now may God grant . . .
       that they may sit down in the kingdom of God;
       yea, and also all those . . .
       that they may go no more out,

but that they may praise him forever.
And may God grant that it may be done
according to my words, even as I have spoken.
Amen.

Individual psalms of lament—unlike communal psalms—conclude with a "vow of trust" or "promise of praise." Alma 29:17 makes a final request that Alma, his brethren, and their converts will be able to "sit down in the kingdom of God" and "go no more out" and promises to "praise him forever." Some scholars say this vow is inappropriate bargaining with God, suggesting that this is an attempt to trade praise for blessings. If this vow of praise is a bargain, then it was not a wise one. Nothing in Alma's immediate situation changes because he spoke these words. What was a problem is still a problem. This is made dramatically clear when Alma 30 begins by briefly summarizing the same politico-historical situation explained in Alma 28. Nothing has changed in the setting or the circumstances—nothing except, perhaps, Alma himself.

The lament process is not a panacea, though Alma, himself, seems different. The invocation alone reminds psalmists who God is and who they are—and that may reopen a relationship that was damaged or abandoned when pain and trauma descended. Harrowed and harmed, some suffer wordlessly and some cry out in pain, some blame enemies and others blame the God who allowed such suffering to happen. Lament is a choice to cry out to that same God—a miracle no less amazing than prison walls tumbling down.

From a place of quiet where a life has been undone, a psalmist turns to God, searching for God to justify or at least rationalize what has happened. But where is the language that makes meaning of the unspeakable? What can renew a life that has been emptied by circumstances, choices of others, or traumatic events? How can a psalmist live with frightening gaps and silences? A person in pain may speak angry, hateful, hopeless, unforgiveable, God-blaming, enemy-naming words. A person may speak what ought not to be said and admit what ought not to be felt and do so using the words of past prophets who legitimized that articulation in scripture. Powerful words are needed to separate the darkness from the light, to name pain, to identify who is God and the enemy and everyone else, and to dissect the difference between commandments, personal responsibility, and self-accusation. Finding those words is a process.

Alma's angel first appeared with earth-shaking confidence and the thunderous words of God, demanding attention and inducing repentance. In the context of trauma at Ammonihah and repeated rejections and failures during his ministry, Alma's desire to be an angel makes sense. But Alma's wish to be an angel may also be the wish to have his soul separate from his body. Witness to unspeakable horror that left unspeakable pain, Alma later laments, "O, how long, O Lord, wilt thou suffer that thy servants shall dwell here below in the flesh...?" (Alma 31:26). Alma wisely cried these words when others could hear and in a process that ends with praise—though he still chose to circle back and re-cry, "O Lord God, how long...?" (Alma 31:30). Following the rules does not mean a psalmist will end with a tidy resolution or easy healing. The promise of following the structure is simply that lament will end, and it will end in praise.

Alma and Nephi called upon God in personal and familiar terms, leaving a legacy that pushes back against those who unknowingly suggest that there is no room for the hopeless, the abandoned, the broken, the guilty, the damaged, the angry, the bitter.[9] Within the structure of a psalm of lament, there is space for a wounded person to become as a child and ask those childlike questions, Why? and How long? for as long as is needed. There is space for God and others to listen. Asking questions can change the speaker. Hearing them can change the listener.

Asking Why? or How long? in a psalm of lament is not doubt or apostasy; it is poetry. A person who laments is not whining, and a prophet who laments is not weak. People in pain who name their enemies are not unbelieving; they are Nephi. Traumatized people who are not "content with the things which the Lord hath allotted" are not faithless; they are Alma. When Alma had no words, he found his broken voice in Nephi's poetic structure—and both found a path forward from a cycle of self-blaming questions. Re-voicing words is an act of faith that the word of God is alive, that past poetry is present scripture, that a psalmist's ancient words of pain can heal the unhealable—or at least begin to unburden the unbearable.

Poignantly, even Jesus, the Word, used another's words to express his agony on the cross. He lamented in the words of Psalm 22, crying in a "loud voice": "My God, my God, why hast thou forsaken me?" (Matt 27:46).

Silence was the answer.

But that does not mean the question was faithless, worthless, meaningless, or mere complaining. It does not mean the answer was disapproving, judgmental, unresponsive, or without feeling. It means that when the extremities of life stripped words from the Word, Jesus turned to his father as a child, and in the most personal of terms, he asked the most childlike of questions: Why?

Conclusion

Beholding This Scene

The invitation issued in the introduction of this book was to read a few Book of Mormon stories that you have probably read before and see them anew. Whether you are reading these stories and seeing them for the first time or the fortieth time, you will need your eyes open. You rely on your eyesight—and sometimes upon glasses. If you have anything less than perfect vision, then you likely remember the first time you put on glasses. Suddenly the world snapped into sharp lines and crisp edges, and you understood in a moment that what you see is not necessarily what everyone else sees. Something similar happens when you read a story. How you look at a story can change what you see in the story. Putting on the "glasses" of your background or culture, or looking through the "lenses" of your age, gender, or education, will help you interpret the story, but these interpretations are framed by the lenses through which you are looking. The questions you ask predetermine the answers you will most likely find.

What if someone puts on various glasses and looks at the story of Abish? Depending on how radically different the various lenses are from each other, we may find radically different, even contradictory, viewpoints. However, often we find different but complementary interpretations. We might view Abish's story through the lens of social justice issues, or query her story about gender, or consider possible symbolic interpretation. Asking different questions is like putting on different glasses. Those glasses are perspectives that highlight different aspects and pull them into view.

story

Two missionary brothers, Ammon and Aaron, and a few others bring the gospel message to two culturally and religiously hostile kings, a father and a son, both of whom are married to strong and independent Lamanite queens. Words, actions, and reactions align between the two stories largely because Aaron is converted to Ammon's approach. Both kings pray and fall to the earth, seeming as if they are dead (Alma 18:42; 22:18). The plots diverge when the queens react differently: the father's wife is angry and wants her servants to kill the missionary who taught her husband (Alma 22:19), while the son's wife is devastated and remains by his side (Alma 18:43). Lamoni arises just long enough to reach for his wife, call her blessed, and swear on her life that he has seen his Redeemer before "[sinking] again with joy" (Alma 19:13). The queen falls down as well and is followed shortly by the rest of the household, all appearing "as though they were dead" (verse 18). The single person in Lamoni's household who does not fall is a servant named Abish. She runs to get the townspeople, but instead of being amazed by the miracle, they start bickering (verses 16–19). One man draws "his sword and [goes] forth that he might let it fall upon Ammon," but he falls down dead instead (verse 22). Worried that the bickering may turn into full-fledged violence, Abish takes the queen's hand, and the queen arises (verse 29). The queen takes the king's hand, and he arises, quickly stepping in to calm the crowd (verses 30–31). Readers never hear of Abish again.

117

introduction 1: social justice and equality

Though mentioned in only a few verses in a single chapter of the Book of Mormon, Abish is the lynchpin of this story, which is surprising considering that she is a low-ranking person in every sense. She is a woman in a book that names only six women, three of whom are named merely as biblical allusions, rather than women in their own story. Having been converted "many years" ago, Abish is probably somewhat older in a society that rarely speaks of the elderly. Perhaps being the queen's servant gives her some status, but she is still a servant, and, moreover, she is not even a "Lamanite" servant but a "Lamanitish" servant. Readers are never told what it means to be Lamanitish, though it seems probable that Abish is not a Lamanite or a Nephite. In a book that categorizes nearly everyone, Abish resists being labeled as one or the other, and, instead, falls somewhere in the middle. The story hints that this is not an enviable position; king Lamoni has no problem killing his "Lamanitish" servants over minor infractions that were not their fault.

Abish has yet another identity that classifies her. Though she has never "made it known," Abish was "converted unto the Lord for many years, on account of a remarkable vision of her father" (Alma 19:17, 16), wording that leaves her conversion story open to interpretation. Did Abish see a remarkable vision of her father, which converted her to the Lord? Or did her father see a remarkable vision, which converted her to the Lord? Either way, this woman is a believer who never speaks of her belief, suggesting that being labeled as a believer would not be viewed in a positive light—yet one more reason she has lower standing in her society.

introduction 2: gender relations, sensory perception and perspective

Abish not only sees clearly but is, for a time, the only person who sees at all. This moment in which Abish sees draws the reader's attention to perspective—with striking implications. From whose point of view do readers "see" this story? Even if Ammon told everything he knew, he is not the source of information in Alma 19:14–32. He cannot be; he is lying prostrate on the ground, "overpowered with joy," as are the queen and the king (verses 13–14), and all the servants (verse 16). There is only one person who knows what happened next: Abish. At very least, Alma 19:16–17 is from Abish's perspective. These few verses explain Abish's conversion, then describe Abish's decision to gather the people, hoping that in "beholding this scene" the townspeople will begin to "believe in the power of God" (verse 17). No one else knows about her conversion, no one else witnesses what happens when the whole household is on the ground, and no one else can explain her inner thoughts. The phrasing and word choice support the theory that Abish is the source and perhaps even the voice of (at least) the one and a half verses about her conversion. From the first mention of her name through Alma 19:17, what happens with words and originality is stunning.

In these verses, there are eight words or phrases that are completely unique, two phrases that are not used elsewhere in the Book of Mormon, and eight more phrases that are only used in the Book of Mormon but only used after Abish's story (see FIGURE 10). That so many phrases are unique or first used by Abish suggests a fascinating possibility: these are Abish's words. No one else speaks like this in scripture. It is not unreasonable to suggest that the narrator/author/editor simply

119

switched a few pronouns and wrote "Abish" instead of "I"—and then quoted the rest: I, Abish, "having been converted unto the Lord for many years, on account of a remarkable vision of [my] father..." (verse 16).

Could such a thing be possible? Mormon speaks openly about other records when he explains how he cannot write even "a hundredth part of the proceedings of this people, yea, the account of the Lamanites and of the Nephites" (Hel. 3:14). The account of the Lamanites is listed first because Mormon is referring back to a statement about Anti-Nephi-Lehi record keeping: "And now there are many records kept of the proceedings of this people, by many of this people, which are particular and very large, concerning them" (Hel. 3:13). In this context, the word "particular" can mean "pertaining to a single person."[1] That the Anti-Nephi-Lehies are specifically singled out as copious record keepers does not say Abish kept a record, but it does enliven the prospect. She could be one of the particular people who kept a particular record.

ABISH: SYMBOLIC REALITY AND
THE PLAN OF SALVATION
introduction 3: cultural and religious symbolism
Abish's story is told straightforwardly, and yet there are indications that it should also be read on a symbolic level. The complex relationship between what is real and what is symbolic is demonstrated in this story with the pervasive theme of falling. After Ammon teaches of the "creation of Adam" and "all the things concerning the fall of man" (Alma 18:36; my emphasis), teachings that are replicated in increasing detail by Aaron for King Lamoni's father (see Alma 22:12–14), Lamoni collapses on the ground, rises momentarily on the third day, and then falls to the earth again, followed by the queen, then Ammon, and then the rest of the people

120

in the world of Lamoni's household. Except for Abish, every person in the household physically "[falls] unto the earth" (Alma 18:42). Besides those who collapse and appear to be dead, the word fall is used to describe those who are killed or who may be killed (Alma 17:36; 19:24; 20:17; 22:19; and 22:20), people who are captured (Alma 17:20; 20:30), and, strangely, even the way that the man uses his sword to try to kill Ammon, namely by "let[ting] it fall upon Ammon, to slay him" (Alma 19:22). The abundant use of fall highlights how many people fall, as well as when, why, and how they fall. Those details in turn focus readers on the stunning difference between falling down dead and falling down as if dead, and between falling physically and falling spiritually.

Oddly, the townspeople are not worried that they will "fall" dead like the man who attempted to kill Ammon. They are, instead, afraid of touching the dead bodies around them (see Alma 19:24). According to Mosaic law, touching a dead body renders a person unclean or defiled for seven days. If this is why the people are afraid, then it would make sense that Abish would know the law and its consequences. Touching the queen is risking what little status she has. Nevertheless, Abish "went and took the queen by the hand, that perhaps she might raise her from the ground; and as soon as she touched her hand she arose and stood upon her feet" (Alma 19:29). Abish's mere touch raises the queen from a physical deathlike state—but she speaks as if she has been awakened from a spiritually dead state, declaring, "O blessed Jesus, who has saved me from an awful hell! O blessed God, have mercy on this people" (verse 29). The queen does not sound as if she has been helped up from a fall, but as if she has been saved from *the fall*.

Symbolically, Abish raises the queen from spiritual and physical death. Notably, the queen imitates Abish's

used only in Book of Mormon, used by Abish first	not used anywhere else in scripture
converted unto the Lord	converted to the Lord
making known unto the people	converted… for many years
what had happened	remarkable
beholding this scene	never having made it known
cause them to believe	
ran forth	lay prostrate
ran forth from house to house	lay prostrate upon the earth
making it known unto the people	supposing that this opportunity

used elsewhere in scripture, but not in Book of Mormon

vision of [her father]	mistress

FIGURE 10 Abish's words (Alma 19:16–17)

life-giving process precisely: once she has arisen, the queen "[takes] the king, Lamoni, by the hand," and the king then "[arises] and [stands] upon his feet" (verse 30). The repetition and the precision of this phrasing should tell readers to notice this moment. Why hands? Why clarity about both the briefness of the touch and the quickness of the response? Just because something is written realistically does not preclude the same words from being interpreted symbolically.

conclusion 1: social justice and equality

Had she not been "converted unto the Lord for many years, on account of a remarkable vision of her father" and thereafter maintained her quiet faith (Alma 19:16), Abish would not have been ready when the Lord needed her. She plays a crucial role in gathering the people. Moreover, she had the courage to touch the queen's hand and help her to arise, thus allowing the "work of the Lord" to "commence among the Lamanites" (verse 36). In a time when there is frustration about a text with so few women, readers find the story of a woman who does not have the social capital to be noticed, but she is; she should not have the power to change anything, but she does.

How does Abish do it? It is not power from a typical social hierarchy. Abish is in the right place at the right time, but there is more: who she is allows her to stand although everyone else has fallen and although she is an underprivileged, supposedly powerless woman. Abish sees as clearly as Ammon does, and she keeps her wits when he falls to the earth and even when the crowd is on the verge of rioting. What does it take to see as clearly as Abish? What does it take to behold people and recognize the power of God inside of them despite outward appearances?

The story of king Lamoni and his father is about conversion and kings, about missionaries and mercy, but it is also the story of Abish. With a past comprised of one event (her conversion) and a present in which she is present for a mere handful of verses, Abish is of no consequence in all the ways that seem to matter most. But God sees her, and she sees God's power. She has no future in the Book of Mormon, but Abish changes her world in the few moments she is present.

conclusion 2: gender relations,
sensory perception, and perspective

Even when a story is written with third-person pronouns, point of view impacts the reader. Readers tend
to sympathize with the character from whose perspective the story is told. Some likely question the ability of point of view to do such work. If all characters
are referred to as he or she, how can one perspective
dominate and garner more empathy? There are actually numerous ways, but perhaps a simple example
will help: How many people remember Ammah and
Muloki when they finish the Book of Mormon? How
many remember Abish? Ammah and Muloki are actually named twice (see Alma 20:2; 21:11), while Abish
is named once (Alma 19:16). Readers may notice her
because she is a woman, because they empathize with
her plight, because she reacts so vigorously, or because
they are unconsciously drawn to her. All of those occur
in part because of point of view. We remember Abish
because we think her thoughts for a few verses. We
may even speak Abish's personal words.

If these are her words, they have been hidden in
plain view—a metaphor that is appropriate for Abish.
Abish seems silent—so silent that readers may wonder
why she deserves to be one of the few named women.
Her words are voiced by the narrator and integrated
into an ongoing epic in readable third-person prose,
similar to the many individuals who are subsumed
when history is painted with broad brushstrokes. Yet
even when readers did not know they were hearing
her words, they were affected. Abish's voice is authentic and uniquely her own. What she thought and said
remains imprinted on the Book of Mormon in a story
that is perhaps just beginning to be heard. Readers

remember her not only because they hear her but also because they see the story through her eyes—and that is a privilege to behold because Abish sees clearly. She knows what the power of God looks like when she sees it. Her words speak for her and in behalf of other people who have little claim to what the world calls power.

ABISH: SYMBOLIC REALITY AND
THE PLAN OF SALVATION

conclusion 3: cultural and religious symbolism

Abish's actions courageously challenge religious practices and biblical law, and likely challenge gender, age, cultural and socioeconomic expectations, as well. They also challenge readers in another way: if read symbolically, Abish is a Christ figure.[2] As Christ is both divine and human, unable to be categorized as one or the other and hence able to complete his unique mission, Abish is also in a unique position as a Lamanitish woman. She bridges the cultural and religious space between the Nephite church and the Lamanites when Ammon brings the fall to this household and then falls, himself; she bridges socioeconomic space between the royalty and the people when she calls the people to come to the royal court; and she bridges life and death when she gives life to the queen, and the queen gives life to the king. In the heart of a book troubled by war and regular (doubtless hand-to-hand) combat, Abish shares life and the queen receives life, hand-to-hand. The symbolism challenges readers to consider what their hands do. Do they destroy or bring life? bridge divides or increase the gap? help others arise or let them remain fallen? Though she has no power and no status in this world, Abish can symbolically raise the dead, doing so with such fullness that a mere touch changes people into life-givers, themselves. Like Christ, Abish has nothing; she descends below everyone else in this story, yet her quiet conversion allows her to lift people when they fall to the earth—and to do so powerfully and with abundance.

* * *

The most important question to ask when analyzing Abish's story, or any story, may not be, "What does this story mean?" but, rather, "What else does this story mean?"[3]

That question is why I might be wrong but also why I might be right and why this book—this series—is important. I might be mistaken about Alma's wickedness, his affinity with Nehor, or his trauma at Ammonihah, and I might be wrong about mourning, righteousness, Nephi, or lamentation. My conclusions should be questioned. And yet to question my conclusions, you will need to read scripture. Whether you agree or disagree with my interpretation of scripture, I consider my efforts a success if you have begun or renewed your commitment to studying the Book of Mormon.

Many people have many questions. Real questions can be great and terrible. My personal experience is that Book of Mormon verses do not answer all these questions. I read it, and the answers to my questions were not there. Only on one occasion have I randomly opened the Book of Mormon, looked down, and found my eyes resting on a verse that answered an immediate, pressing concern. The answers people give in scripture and in life can be shallow and unsatisfying. That is not a reason to doubt scripture. We may be asking the wrong questions, looking for the wrong answers. While God cares about our personal questions, he might know that a different answer to a different question is what is most needed.

Abish thought she could bring the people to king Lamoni's house and that there, "by beholding this scene it would cause them to believe in the power of God" (Alma 19:17). She thought if she provided the answer that they would see. But she was wrong. They could not behold the answer because they were not asking that question. How can they—or we—understand God's powerful answers if we do not ask the questions he is answering? The Book of Mormon has life-changing answers to some questions—and those questions are priceless. Nevertheless, the process of searching for the questions means reading these stories, which will likely multiply your Why? and your How long? questions. This is also not a reason to doubt scripture. Questions are not sinful. Scripture asks and provokes more fearful and faithless questions than I have ever thought of asking. That is one of the many reasons why it is good to read the word of God.

The questions are some of the reasons why we need these stories now and why reading them deeply will change you. Reading has changed me. I am not the same person who began studying Alma years ago.

I thought I knew his story then. I think I do now. But reading again could change that again. Until it does, my current perspective is this: Alma does not want to be your hero. He uses inclusive plural pronouns when talking to Ammonihah's citizens about those of us who "have hardened our hearts against the word." He says that we will wish "we could command the rocks and the mountains to fall upon us to hide us from [God's] presence" (Alma 12:13–14). Alma knows how it feels to stare into the abyss of his own most terrible, unfixable mistakes. For any blessed moment of quiet peace, he praises and glorifies God, never himself.

Ammonihah remains deeply troubling to me. I remember the day I finally saw the chief judge's *schadenfreude*, ☞ the women and children, the anguish of Alma and Amulek, that horrible fire. I am not the same. How can one approach such stories? These stories will break your heart and crush your spirit.[4] But Jesus commands us to come unto him with "a broken heart and a contrite spirit" (3 Ne. 12:19). Why he wants broken people is a question worth asking. It is also a warning: Reading the word of God is risky. Reading about Abish, Alma, or Ammonihah will hurt. You should be broken in some degree by their brokenness, crushed in your own small ways by their pain. In reading of Abish, you live a quiet life, a hidden, overlooked, converted life, and then you wait for years for God to need you. With Alma, you awaken and find you are miraculously healed to the degree you were hurting. And then you awake again the next morning and every morning, discovering that the pain and past are still present everywhere. Nothing has changed, nothing but you. If you dare to read about the fires of Ammonihah, you may never recover.

☞ This German word refers to finding pleasure or joy in another's pain. There is no English equivalent.

The stories of scripture can be difficult to read for some of the same reasons why we need to engage deeply. Paying the price to understand these stories also calls us to genuinely see and suffer, but therein lies hope. In my interpretation, Alma's story of sin and sorrow says this: You are not the first person in the darkest abyss. Repent. When the pain of sin comes around again, choose to cry out for mercy again. The war in Alma 28 and the faithfulness of the Anti-Nephi-Lehies says this: Others have been troubled, pained, and exceedingly sorrowful. Mourn with those who mourn. Mourn more truly with those who truly mourn. Ammonihah says this: A high priest of the church of God understands how it feels to be victimized, to be traumatized, to be silenced. When you can, speak in your own words and with your own voice. If you cannot find the words that express the unspeakable, borrow some from Nephi or Alma. Lament what needs lamenting. Behold what needs beholding. Weep when others are weeping, and grieve when you need healing. Read these stories. Write your particular story. Sing "O that I were an angel." Behold the power of God.

Further Reading

literary approaches to scripture

Hardy, Grant. *Understanding the Book of Mormon: A Reader's Guide.* New York: Oxford University Press, 2010. This study edition of the Book of Mormon includes many features that help the reader to identify literary devices and structures of the text as well as to make connections to other parts of scripture. Grant Hardy has restructured the text to be in original paragraph form, or in poetic structure when appropriate. It has footnotes for clarifying chronological order, which may be particularly helpful in the book of Alma. The following pages are most relevant: 115–19, 132–42, 148–51, 170–74, 308–9. Notes 28–30 are also helpful.

Lehnen, Christine. "Exploring Narratives' Powers of Emotional Persuasion through Character Involvement: A Working Heuristic." *Journal of Literary Theory* 10, no. 2 (2016): 247–70. This article reviews the psychological and literary research on the emotional and persuasive effects of narratives. Narratives use the transformational power of emotion to invite and persuade the reader to change their mind.

Miller-McLemore, Bonnie J., ed. *The Wiley-Blackwell Companion to Practical Theology.* Chichester, UK: Wiley-Blackwell, 2014. This guide discusses how theology need not be deeply philosophical but should instead be focused on real-life struggles and everyday activities of faith. It suggests that if theology is not practical, it is not meaningful.

Parry, Donald W. *Poetic Parallelisms in the Book of Mormon: The Complete Text Reformatted*. Provo, UT: Neal A. Maxwell Institute for Religious Scholarship, 2007. https://scholarsarchive.byu.edu/cgi/viewcontent.cgi?article=1060&context=mi. This is a fantastic resource for understanding the wide variety of poetic parallel forms in the Book of Mormon. It contains detailed definitions, descriptions, and examples of different types of parallelisms to familiarize the reader with the purposes of these poetic forms. It contains the entire text of the Book of Mormon formatted in a way that highlights each unique parallel form in a recognizable way.

Rust, Richard Dilworth. *Feasting on the Word: The Literary Testimony of the Book of Mormon*. Salt Lake City, UT: Deseret Book, 1997. Rust beautifully documents the ways in which taking a literary approach to studying the Book of Mormon strengthens one's testimony of its divinity and masterful construction. He explains how the poetic devices, style, tone, narrative structure, word choice, and so on, all contribute to the reader having a spiritual experience with the text and being able to feast upon the words of Christ.

Ryken, Leland. "The Bible as Literature." In *The Origin of the Bible*, edited by Phillip W. Comfort. Carol Stream, IL: Tyndale House, 2013, 111–52. Ryken argues that to draw meaningful interpretations and conclusions from scripture, it should be studied and approached as literature.

Ska, Jean Louis. *"Our Fathers Have Told Us": Introduction to the Analysis of Hebrew Narratives*. Rome: Editrice Pontificio Istituto Biblico, 1990.

Ska discusses the literary criticism method of narratology and gives examples of how this method can be used to explore narratives in scripture.

Sperry, Sidney B. "Types of Literature in the Book of Mormon: Epistles, Psalms, Lamentations." *Journal of Book of Mormon Studies* 4, no. 1 (1995): 69–80. Sperry identifies and analyzes the epistles, psalms, and lamentations in the Book of Mormon. He explains why 2 Nephi 4:16–35 is classified as a psalm in both form and idea.

Yamasaki, Gary. *Perspective Criticism: Point of View and Evaluative Guidance in Biblical Narrative*. Eugene, OR: Cascade Books, 2012. Yamasaki artfully explains the importance of point of view in scriptural narratives. He compares narrator perspective to the camera's view in films, making the concepts he expounds upon accessible and relatable.

Zeelander, Susan. *Closure in Biblical Narrative*. Leiden: Brill, 2011. Zeelander analyzes the devices biblical authors used to communicate closure at the end of a narrative. Her discussion on framing, summaries, and rituals may be of most interest in the context of studying the Book of Alma.

Alma

Belnap, Daniel. "'And he was Anti-Christ': The Significance of the Eighteenth Year of the Reign of the Judges, Part 2." *Journal of Book of Mormon Studies* 28 (2019): 91–136. This article and its predecessor focus on the social, political, and philosophical contexts leading up to and through the eighteenth year of the reign of the judges, during which Alma sermonizes to the Zoramites, teaches his sons, and disappears.

Clark, John L. "Painting Out the Messiah: The Theologies of Dissidents." *Journal of Book of Mormon Studies* 11, no. 1 (2002): 16–27. This article gives an overview of dissenting voices in the Book of Mormon and their corresponding reasoning and beliefs. It covers, among other things, the interactions between Alma and Nehor, Amlici, and Korihor. It may be of interest to consider Alma's powerful words to and about prominent unbelievers after considering his own past as an unbeliever.

Conkling, J. Christopher. "Alma's Enemies: The Case of the Lamanites, Amlicites, and Mysterious Amalekites." *Journal of Book of Mormon Studies* 14, no. 1 (2005): 109–32. Conkling argues for a theory that Amlicites and Amalekites could actually be referring to the same group of people. If true, this theory would dramatically change the reading and structure of the book of Alma, considering that the record of Alma begins and ends with problems related to this group.

Hull, Kerry M., Nicholas J. Frederick, and Hank Smith, eds. *Give Ear to My Words: Text and Context of Alma 36–42.* Provo, UT: Religious Studies Center, 2019. This book is a collection of essays given at a BYU Sidney B. Sperry Symposium with a focus on chapters 36–42 of the book of Alma. This diverse group of scholars delve into the context that precedes the doctrinal teachings of Alma.

Spencer, Joseph M. "The Structure of the Book of Alma." *Journal of Book of Mormon Studies* 26 (2017): 273–83. Spencer provides striking evidence that suggests that the entire book of Alma has an overarching structure. He argues that considering the parallels in this structure can uncover an important guide to theological intent in the book of Alma.

Turley, Kylie. "Alma's Hell: Repentance, Consequence, and the Lake of Fire and Brimstone." *Journal of Book of Mormon Studies* 28 (2019): 1–45. This article analyzes the disturbing context of Ammonihah that informs many of the theological interpretations in this book. The context of Ammonihah informs the reader about Alma's potential connection to other unbelievers, Alma's personal trauma resulting from the burning of innocent believers, and much more.

Welch, John W. "The Trial of Nehor." In *The Legal Cases in the Book of Mormon*, 211–36. Provo, UT: BYU Press and Neal A. Maxwell Institute for Religious Scholarship, 2008. Welch analyzes Nehor's trial in great depth according to biblical law. He estimates that Alma was in his mid-thirties. Welch speculates that Gideon's words may have constituted a formal legal warning to Nehor from the church, which helps to explain Nehor's over-reactive behavior.

mourning

Anderson, Gary A. *A Time to Mourn, A Time to Dance: The Expression of Grief and Joy in Israelite Religion*. University Park: Pennsylvania State University Press, 1991. Mourning and joy are discussed, not as vague emotions but instead as states of being associated with particular rituals and actions. Biblical narratives suggest that these rituals were prescribed for certain situations and times, and included both individual and communal aspects.

Goff, Alan. "Mourning, Consolation, and Repentance at Nahom." *In Rediscovering the Book of Mormon,* edited by John L. Sorenson and Melvin J. Thorne, 92–99. Provo, UT: Foundation for Ancient Research and Mormon Studies, 1991. This article considers the Hebrew translation of Nahom and how it changes the context and depth of Lehi's family's experiences in the wilderness.

Lambert, David. "Fasting as a Penitential Rite: A Biblical Phenomenon?" *Harvard Theological Review* 96, no. 4 (2003): 477–512. www.jstor.org/stable/4151868. Fasting, as discussed in this article, emphasizes affliction, mourning, and pleading. Both the penitential and nonpenitential nature of biblical fasting are analyzed.

Pham, Xuan Huong Thi. "Mourning in the Ancient Near East and the Hebrew Bible." *Journal for the Study of the Old Testament*. Supplement Series 302. Sheffield, UK: Sheffield Academic Press, 1999. This book describes ancient Near Eastern mourning rites, especially focusing on the practice of lamentations.

psalms of lament

Alford, Kenneth L., and D. Bryce Baker. "Parallels between Psalms 25–31 and the Psalm of Nephi." *In Ascending the Mountain of the Lord: Temple, Praise, and Worship in the Old Testament,* edited by David R. Seely, Jeffrey R. Chadwick, and Matthew J. Grey, 312–28. Salt Lake City, UT: Deseret Book and Religious Studies Center, 2013. This article discusses literary parallels between 2 Nephi 4 and Psalms 25–31, noting the use of enemies among many other similarities.

Alter, Robert. *The Art of Biblical Poetry.* New York: Basic Books, 1985. Chapter Five, "Forms of Faith in Psalms," is particularly helpful in understanding the importance of the poetic medium of psalm in a writer's ability to convey passionate faith in a compact but simple way.

Brueggemann, Walter. "The Costly Loss of Lament." *Journal for the Study of the Old Testament* 36 (1986): 57–71. Brueggemann artfully depicts what we as a community of faith risk losing when we neglect psalms of lament and the important role lament plays in the process of worship. He suggests that lament is a way to redistribute power in a covenant relationship and to engage God in crisis and sorrow instead of just in praise and joy.

Gunkel, Hermann, and Joachim Begrich. *Introduction to Psalms: The Genres of the Religious Lyric of Israel.* Translated by James D. Nogaslski. Macon, GA: Mercer University Press, 1998. Gunkel, the founder of form criticism, is an influential scholar in the field of psalm analysis, and his introductory book provides a detailed guide to understanding and appreciating psalms of lament.

Mandolfo, Carleen. *God in the Dock: Dialogic Tension in the Psalms of Lament.* New York: Sheffield Academic Press, 2002. Mandolfo explores the phenomena of voicing, illogical content, and mood shifts in psalms. It is suggested that understanding different voices and speakers within a psalm can bring a more nuanced analysis of the text.

Nickerson, Matthew. "Nephi's Psalm: 2 Nephi 4:16–35 in the Light of Form-Critical Analysis." *Journal of Book of Mormon Studies* 6, no. 2 (1997): 26–42. Nickerson uses Hermann Gunkel's structure to identify 2 Nephi 4 as a psalm of lament. He argues that understanding the poetic form can bring great personal insights.

Westermann, Claus. *Praise and Lament in the Psalms.* Translated by Keith R. Crim and Richard N. Soulen. Atlanta: John Knox Press, 1981. Westermann analyzes the aspects of praise and lament in biblical psalms, and documents the typical movement from supplication to praise in most psalms of lament. This is a fantastic source for better understanding the literary structure of psalms and the various elements that comprise them.

Westermann, Claus. *The Psalms: Structure, Content and Message.* Minneapolis: Augsburg, 1980. Westermann details the different types and collections of psalms in the Old Testament and helps the reader understand the important context of community psalms of lament.

trauma and psalms of lament

Dickie, June F. "The Intersection of Biblical Lament and Psychotherapy in the Healing of Trauma Memories." *Old Testament Essays* 32, no. 3 (2019): 885–907. This article provides empirical evidence supporting the theory that the biblical form of psalms of lament can help modern-day sufferers express and work through their own pain.

———. "Lament as a Contributor to the Healing of Trauma: An Application of Poetry in the Form of Biblical Lament." *Pastoral Psychology* 68, no. 2 (2018): 145–56. Dickie describes the physiological, psychological, and spiritual effects of trauma and outlines the way in which a biblical lament structure can be used to promote healing. She recounts a fascinating study of Zulu youth who had experienced trauma and were then taught to use the lament structure to express their feelings.

Fewell, Danna N., and Daniel L. Smith-Christopher. "Biblical Lamentations and Singing the Blues." In *Oxford Handbook of Biblical Narrative* edited by Danna Nolan Fewell. New York: Oxford University Press, 2016. Lamentation is compared to African-American blues traditions in their common ability to help individuals process traumatic experiences and return to a sense of self.

Hall, M. Elizabeth Lewis. "Suffering in God's Presence: The Role of Lament in Transformation." *Journal of Spiritual Formation & Soul Care* 9, no. 2 (2016): 219–32. This source explains the psychological concepts behind lament. The lament structure allows the writer to make meaning out of their experiences and transform their emotions from distress to praise.

Neimeyer, Robert A., Olga Herrero, and Luis Botella. "Chaos to Coherence: Psychotherapeutic Integration of Traumatic Loss." *Journal of Constructivist Psychology* 19, no. 2 (2006): 127–45. This research indicates that trauma has a disruptive effect on an individual's personal narrative. The authors suggest psychotherapeutic techniques to address this narrative disruption and bring back coherence into an individual's post-trauma life.

Orange, Donna M. "Speaking the Unspeakable: 'The Implicit,' Traumatic Living Memory, and the Dialogue of Metaphors." *International Journal of Psychoanalytic Self-Psychology* 6, no. 2 (2011): 187–206. Orange argues that dualities such as body versus mind, conscious versus unconscious, and verbal versus nonverbal, are better understood as being on a continuum. Metaphor may be a means that allows the "unspeakable" to be spoken in some degree.

women in scripture

Berkey, Kimberly M., and Joseph M. Spencer, "'Great Cause to Mourn': The Complexity of The Book of Mormon's Presentation of Gender and Race," In *Americanist Approaches to the Book of Mormon* edited by Elizabeth Fenton and Jared Hickman, 273–283. New York: Oxford University Press, 2019. Berkey and Spencer argue compellingly that the Book of Mormon is self-critical about gender. Based on Jacob's sermon in Jacob 2–3, the authors argue that the Nephite history is largely one of oppressing women, while Lamanites in the few stories told have egalitarian and loving familial and gender relations.

Smith, Hannah Clayson. "Protecting the Widows and the Fatherless in the Book of Mormon." *Studia Antiqua* 3, no. 2 (2003); 173–80. https://scholarsarchive.byu.edu/studiaantiqua/vol3/iss2/9. This article analyzes the special protections given to widows and the fatherless according to biblical law and explores how these special protections extend into Book of Mormon societies.

Williams, Camille. "Women in the Book of Mormon." *Journal of Book of Mormon Studies* 11; 66–79, 111–14 no. 1 (2002). https://scholarsarchive.byu.edu/jbms/vol11/iss1/12. Williams examines potential reasons for why women are not more prominent in the Book of Mormon text. She likewise suggests why readers should pause before categorizing the Book of Mormon as a misogynistic book of men's witnesses, using the story of Abish to justify this invitation.

Endnotes

SERIES INTRODUCTION

1. Elder Neal A. Maxwell, "The Children of Christ," university devotional, Brigham Young University, Provo, UT, 4 February 1990, https://speeches.byu.edu/talks/neal-a-maxwell_children-christ/.

2. Elder Neal A. Maxwell, "The Inexhaustible Gospel," university devotional, Brigham Young University, Provo, UT, 18 August 1992, https://speeches.byu.edu/talks/neal-a-maxwell/ inexhaustible-gospel/.

3. Elder Neal A. Maxwell, "The Book of Mormon: A Great Answer to 'The Great Question,'" address, Book of Mormon Symposium, Brigham Young University, Provo, UT, 10 October 1986, reprinted in *The Voice of My Servants: Apostolic Messages on Teaching, Learning, and Scripture,* ed. Scott C. Esplin and Richard Neitzel Holzapfel (Provo, UT: Religious Studies Center, Brigham Young University; Salt Lake City: Deseret Book, 2010), 221–38, https://rsc.byu.edu/archived/ voice-my-servants/book-mormon-great-answer-great-question.

INTRODUCTION

1. Christine Lehnen, "Exploring Narratives' Powers of Emotional Persuasion through Character Involvement: A Working Heuristic," *Journal of Literary Theory* 10, no. 2 (2016): 247–70.

2. While I am responsible for my interpretations, I am grateful for the invaluable help of Hannah Van Woerkom, Benjamin Spencer, Sydney Baker, and Macy Larson, and editorial support by Kristine Haglund, Jim Faulconer, Miranda Wilcox, and the staff at the Maxwell Institute.

PART I

1. This constitutes 7.4 percent of the Book of Mormon, making Alma the third author (behind Mormon and Nephi) in terms of personal word count. See Wayne A. Larsen, Alvin C. Rencher, and Tim Layton, "Who Wrote the Book of Mormon? An Analysis of Wordprints," *BYU Studies Quarterly* 20, no. 2 (1980): 246, https://scholarsarchive.byu.edu/ byusq/vol20/iss3/2.

2. Susan Zeelander, *Closure in Biblical Narrative*, vol. 111. (Leiden: Brill, 2012) 200.

1

1. This estimate is in the footnotes of editions of the Book of Mormon published before 2013. Conkling also believes that Alma's conversion is "less than a decade old" when first year of the reign of the judges commences. See J. Christopher Conkling, "Alma's Enemies: The Case of the Lamanites, Amlicites, and Mysterious Amalekites," *Journal of Book of Mormon Studies* (1992–2007) 14, no. 1 (2005): 114¬–15. John Welch estimates that Alma is in his mid-thirties during Nehor's trial. See John W. Welch, "The Trial of Nehor," in The Legal Cases in the Book of Mormon (Provo, UT: BYU Press and Neal A. Maxwell Institute for Religious Scholarship, 2008), 211–36.

2. Robert A. Neimeyer, "Searching for the Meaning of Meaning: Grief Therapy and the Process of Reconstruction," *Death Studies* 24, no. 6 (2000): 541–58.

2

1. The word *chapter* was not on the golden plates, but Joseph Smith saw some sort of break in the text that he called chapters. Apparently intended by their ancient authors, these original chapters are longer and more narrative-based than the chapter breaks in the current Book of Mormon. Orson Pratt created the smaller chapters and the versification in 1879. See Royal Skousen, "Changes in the Book of Mormon," *Interpreter: A Journal of Latter-day Saint Faith and Scholarship* 4 (2011): 161–76.

2. King Mosiah dies in the first year of the reign of the judges, after ruling for thirty-three years. If one to nine years pass between the first year of the reign of the judges and Alma's conversion (footnote estimates, which seem like a relatively good guess), and if the children were between birth and five years of age, then the "children" would be somewhere between twenty-four and thirty-seven years of age when Alma sees the angel.

3. See, for example, Alma 21:8–9 (Amalekites), Alma 30:13–14 (Korihor), and Alma 31:16 (Zoramites).

4. Royal Skousen, *Analysis of Textual Variants* (Provo, UT: The

Foundation for Ancient Research and Mormon Studies, Brigham Young University, 2007): 4:2331.

5. While the wording of the Book of Mormon was "translated into modern speech by the gift and power of God," the punctuation was not. As noted in the Gospel Topics Essay on "Book of Mormon Translation," John Gilbert, an employee at the Grandin Print Shop, "later inserted punctuation marks," since "Joseph Smith did not call for punctuation, such as periods, commas, or question marks as he dictated." "Book of Mormon Translation," *Gospel Topics Essays*, 2016, https://www.churchofjesuschrist.org/manual/gospel-topics-essays/book-of-mormon-translation?lang=eng (accessed 18 September 2019).

6. John L. Clark, "Painting Out the Messiah: The Theologies of Dissidents," *Journal of Book of Mormon Studies* 11, no. 1 (2002): 20.

3

1. Though textual evidence cannot prove conclusively that Alma was the man described in chapters 1 and 2, this chapter will proceed with that interpretation, assuming that viewing preconversion Alma as an unbelieving, very wicked man makes at least as much sense as the stereotype.

2. See J. Christopher Conkling, "Alma's Enemies: The Case of the Lamanites, Amlicites, and Mysterious Amalekites," *Journal of Book of Mormon Studies* (1992–2007) 14, no. 1 (2005): 108–17.

PART II

1. Joseph M. Spencer, "The Structure of the Book of Alma," *Journal of Book of Mormon Studies* 26 (2017): 273–83.

4

1. See Dale A. Lund, Michael S. Caserta, and Margaret F. Dimond, "A Comparison of Bereavement Adjustments Between Mormon and Non-Mormon Older Adults," *Journal of Religion & Aging* 5, no. 1–2 (1989): 75–92.

2. Courtney S. Campbell, "Eschatological Passage: Death as Progress

in the Latter-Day Saints' Tradition," *Ultimate Reality and Meaning* 25, no. 3 (2002): 185–202.

3. See Joseph M. Spencer, "Chapter 6: The women," *1st Nephi: A Brief Theological Introduction* (Provo, UT: Neal A. Maxwell Institute for Religious Scholarship, 2020): 100–115.

4. Noah Webster and Rosalie J. Slater, Noah Webster's *First Edition of an American Dictionary of the English Language* (San Francisco: Foundation for American Christian Education, 1828), s.v. "complaint" and "murmur."

5. Noah Webster and Rosalie J. Slater, *Noah Webster's First Edition of an American Dictionary of the English Language* (San Francisco: Foundation for American Christian Education, 1828), s.v. "mourn."

6. Hermann Gunkel and Joachim Begrich, *Introductions to Psalms: The Genres of the Religious Lyric of Israel*, trans. James P. Nogaslski, (Macon, GA: Mercer University Press, 1998), 84.

7. For example, see Joel 2:12.

8. Kimberly M. Berkey and Joseph M. Spencer, both authors of volumes in this series, argue persuasively that gender relationships are substantially more egalitarian among the Lamanites. See Kimberly M. Berkey and Joseph M. Spencer, "'Great Cause to Mourn': The Complexity of The Book of Mormon's Presentation of Gender and Race," in *Americanist Approaches to the Book of Mormon*, ed. Elizabeth Fenton and Jared Hickman (New York: Oxford University Press, 2019), 273–283.

9. Patriarchal property rights did not apply if a woman was the mother of that heir. Hannah Clayson Smith, "Protecting the Widows and the Fatherless in the Book of Mormon," *Studia Antiqua* 3, no. 2 (2003): 174.

10. See, for example, Mosiah 29:32 and 3 Ne. 6:14–16.

5

1. Robert Alter, *The Art of Biblical Poetry* (New York: Basic Books, 1985).

2. Carl J. Cranney, "The Deliberate Use of Hebrew Parallelisms in the Book of Mormon," *Journal of Book of Mormon Studies* 23 (2014): 140–65.

3. Miranda Wilcox, "*Tender Mercies* in English Idiom and in Nephi's Record," in *A Dream, a Rock, and a Pillar of Fire*, ed. Adam S. Miller

(Provo, UT: Neal A. Maxwell Institute for Religious Scholarship, 2017), 75–110.

4. See also Alma 5:50; 12:15, 29; 13:24; 14:11; 36:28.

5. For Alma's use of "my joy," see Alma 7:5 (two uses); 7:17.

6. Nissim Amzallag and Mikhal Avriel, "Complex Antiphony in Psalms 121, 126 and 128: The Steady Responsa Hypothesis," *Old Testament Essays* 23, no. 3 (2010): 502–18.

7. Carleen Mandolfo, *God in the Dock: Dialogic Tension in the Psalms of Lament*, vol. 357 (New York: Sheffield Academic Press, 2002), 9–10.

8. Mandolfo, *God in the Dock,* 6.

9. See, for example, Bessel A. Van der Kolk, *The Body Keeps the Score: Brain, Mind, and Body in the Healing of Trauma* (New York: Penguin Books, 2015); Mark Wolynn, *It Didn't Start with You: How Inherited Family Trauma Shapes Who We Are and How to End the Cycle* (New York: Viking, 2016); Shelly Rambo, *Spirit and Trauma: A Theology of Remaining* (Louisville: Westminster John Knox Press, 2010); N. Elizabeth Lewis Hall, "Suffering in God's Presence: The Role of Lament in Transformation," *Journal of Spiritual Formation & Soul Care* 9, no. 2 (2016): 219–32; June F. Dickie, "Lament as a Contributor to the Healing of Trauma: An Application of Poetry in the Form of Biblical Lament," *Pastoral Psychology* 68 (2019): 145–56.

6

1. Sidney B. Sperry, "Types of Literature in the Book of Mormon: Epistles, Psalms, Lamentations," *Journal of Book of Mormon Studies* 4, no. 1 (Spring 1995): 77; reprint from Sidney B. Sperry, *Our Book of Mormon* (Salt Lake City: Stevens and Wallis, 1947).

2. Matthew Nickerson, "Nephi's Psalm: 2 Nephi 4:16–35 in the Light of From-Critical Analysis," *Journal of Book of Mormon Studies* 6, no. 2 (1997): 26–42.

3. Claus Westermann, *The Psalms: Structure, Content and Message* (Minneapolis: Augsburg Publishing House, 1980), 61.

4. Alan Lenzi, "Invoking the God: Interpreting Invocations in Mesopotamian Prayers and Biblical Laments of the Individual," *Journal of Biblical Literature* 129, no. 2 (Summer 2010), 313.

5. Walter Brueggemann, "The Costly Loss of Lament," *Journal for the Study of the Old Testament* 36 (1986): 62.

6. Claus Westermann, *Praise and Lament in the Psalms*, trans. Keith R. Crim and Richard N. Soulen (Atlanta: John Knox Press, reprint 1981), 72. See also Westermann, *Praise and Lament*, 74.

7. June F. Dickie, "Lament as a Contributor to the Healing of Trauma: An Application of Poetry in the Form of Biblical Lament," *Pastoral Psychology* 68 (2019): 145–156, doi:10.1007/s11089-018-0851-z.

8. Westermann, *Praise and Lament*, 220.

9. Thomas H. Graves, "The Role of Despair and Anger in Christian Spirituality," *Review and Expositor* 113, no. 2 (2016): 183.

CONCLUSION

1. Noah Webster and Rosalie J. Slater, Noah Webster's First Edition of an American Dictionary of the English Language (San Francisco: Foundation for American Christian Education, 1828), s.v. "particular," http://webstersdictionary1828.com/Dictionary/particular.

2. A former student, Jordan Shumway, drew my attention to this idea.

3. I am indebted to Julie Smith for the succinct phrasing of this idea.

4. See James Strong, "Contrite," in *The New Strong's Expanded Exhaustive Concordance of the Bible* (Nashville: Thomas Nelson Publishers, 2001). Some other Hebrew synonyms for the biblical word translated as *contrite* are "broken or dashed into pieces," crushed, bruised, destroyed, smitten, maimed, and lame.

Index

151

155

Colophon

The text of the book is typeset in Arnhem,
Fred Smeijer's 21st-century-take on late
18th-century Enlightenment-era letterforms
known for their sturdy legibility and clarity
of form. Captions and figures are typset in
Quaadraat Sans, also by Fred Smeijers.
The book title and chapter titles are typeset
in Thema by Nikola Djurek.

Printed on Domtar Lynx 74 gsm,
Forest Stewardship Council (FSC) Certified.

Printed by Brigham Young University Print & Mail Services

Woodcut illuminations Brian Kershisnik
Illumination consultation Faith Heard

Book design & typography Douglas Thomas
Production typesetting Sage Perez, Maria Camargo
Chart design Sage Perez, Douglas Thomas

Alma 19:16 And it came to pass that they did call
on the name of the Lord, in their might, even
until they had all fallen to the earth, save it were
one of the Lamanitish women, whose name
was Abish, she having been converted unto the
Lord for many years, on account of a remarkable
vision of her father.